LEADING WITH HUMILITY

The media is saturated with images of leaders as powerful, headstrong individuals, who are certain of their position and willing to do whatever it takes to achieve their organizational goals or personal ambitions. In reality, far too often, a leader's ego gets in the way of sound decision making, adversely affecting the organization and the individuals involved.

This insightful book, based on cutting edge research, advances a new model for understanding effective leadership. Nielsen, Marrone, and Ferraro advocate the idea of leading with humility, a trait that is rarely discussed and frequently misunderstood. Humble leaders consider their own strengths, weaknesses, and motives in making decisions, demonstrating concern for the common good, and exercising their influence for the benefit of all.

Leading with Humility offers students and leaders clarity in understanding the connection between leadership and humility, and teaches them how to enhance their own abilities to become better leaders.

Rob Nielsen is a Vice President with Jones Lang LaSalle in Seattle, USA.

Jennifer A. Marrone is an Associate Professor in the Department of Management at Seattle University, USA.

Holly S. Ferraro is an Associate Professor in the Department of Management at Seattle University, USA.

LEADING WITH HUMILITY

Rob Nielsen, Jennifer A. Marrone, &
Holly S. Ferraro

Routledge
Taylor & Francis Group

NEW YORK AND LONDON

First published 2014
by Routledge
711 Third Avenue, New York, NY 10017

Simultaneously published in the UK
by Routledge
2 Park Square, Milton Park, Abingdon, Oxon OX14 4RN

Routledge is an imprint of the Taylor & Francis Group, an informa business

Library of Congress Cataloging in Publication Data
Library of Congress Cataloging-in-Publication Data
   Nielsen, Rob.
   Leading with humility / Rob Nielsen, Jennifer A. Marrone, & Holly S. Ferraro.
      pages cm
   Includes bibliographical references and index.
   1. Leadership—Psychological aspects.   2. Humility.   I. Marrone, Jennifer A.   II. Ferraro, Holly S.   III. Title.
   BF637.L4N53 2013
   158'.4—dc23   2012048359

ISBN: 978-0-415-80721-0 (hbk)
ISBN: 978-0-415-80722-7 (pbk)
ISBN: 978-0-203-13953-0 (ebk)

Typeset in Bembo
by RefineCatch Limited, Bungay, Suffolk, UK

Printed and bound in the United States of America by Publishers Graphics, LLC on sustainably sourced paper.

Dedication

Rob dedicates this book to his mom.

Jen dedicates this book to her son, Ryan, who opens her eyes to new perspectives every day.

Holly dedicates this book to the memory of her father, Lorenzo Slay, Sr., who demonstrated loving humility.

About the cover: our book's cover image is meant to evoke feeling. It is intended to prompt questions. In a strikingly similar way, the simple notion to pair leadership with humility has proven provocative, complicated, and unearths contrasting ideas. What does such an image convey about humility, about leadership, about your views of either? The possible interpretations are many and varied.

One might see a leader who has gone down in the trenches, another a leader who walks in another's shoes to experience his or her journey. What do you see? *Leading with Humility* was written for any leader—a business executive, an educational administrator, a company organizer, or you—who wishes to begin the dialogue.

CONTENTS

LIST OF FIGURES AND TABLES

Figures

Tables

ACKNOWLEDGMENTS

We were able to write this book in large part because of the research that came before it. We are indebted and most grateful to all of the authors who are referenced in the pages that follow. Thank you for your work to extend the research in your respective fields of interest.

We would like to acknowledge members of three local businesses and non-profits that shared their perspectives on leading with humility with us. Specifically, we thank Danielle Burd and John Swanson of Umpqua Bank, Mark Secord and Melanie Kristoferson of Neighborcare Health, and Linda Ruthruff and Jesse Davis of Street Bean Espresso. The time we spent with you helped us to learn more about exercising humble leadership in practical and meaningful ways.

Finally, we would like to thank Sharon Golan, Manjula Raman, and the rest of our Routledge team for believing in this project, shepherding us through the process, and their patience while we extended the timeline on several occasions.

Rob Nielsen's Additional Acknowledgments

I would like to note a special thanks to Jim and Cynthia van de Erve for all of their ad hoc editing on numerous papers over the years. I am also grateful to my family for their support and encouragement. In particular, I would like to thank James, Alex, Helen, Uncle Don, Mickey, Mike, Erika, Ruby, and their significant others. Jessica, you hold a unique place in my heart.

I would also like to acknowledge Hans Esterhuizen, Steve Coppess, and Morgan Nilson not only for being incredibly dear friends with whom I have shared many memorable stories and laughs, but also for their valuable insights on different parts of this book.

Over the years, I have been blessed with a number of exceptional business mentors who have taken me under their wing and made it possible for me to have more incredible opportunities than I can count. Thank you to all of you. While writing this book, I returned time and time again to my fond memories of being mentored and learning from Dr. Nick Vidalakis and his wonderful wife, Nancy. Dr. Nick, thank you for your inspiration and please know that I recall your sage advice often.

Finally, thank you Jen and Holly. For everything. When I was an undergraduate in a management fundamentals class at Seattle University and Jen was the professor, she invited and challenged me to develop some thoughts I shared on humility and leadership further. This is where we ended up. I would like to invite and challenge professors everywhere to motivate and encourage their students, even ones with average test scores like me, to do more than is required by the syllabus.

Jennifer A. Marrone's Additional Acknowledgments

I wish to acknowledge and thank Seattle University for granting me a research fellowship that helped to support my efforts in writing this book. I also thank Henny Yun, Tuomi Shen, and Robert Sarver for their research support. I thank and appreciate both of my co-authors for their dedication and wisdom throughout each book writing phase. I have learned a great deal from both of you. And lastly, my deepest gratitude goes to my husband, Sean, who encouraged me to do this in the first place.

Holly S. Ferraro's Additional Acknowledgments

Like Rob and Jen, I am grateful to a number of people for their help and support including people mentioned previously such as Henny Yun. Henny, you went above and beyond the call each time we presented a task. It was a pleasure to work with you. Jen and Rob, thank you for allowing me to be a part of the team. I've appreciated the stimulating discussions that have shaped not just this book, but also my ideas on what it means to collaborate with others. You are both wonderful co-authors. Finally, I thank my husband, Mike Ferraro, for his support. Thanks for talking about ideas with me at dinner, in the car, walking to the mailbox ... I know you probably got sick of hearing about humility but you engaged in talking about it anyway. You are the king of active listening!

PART I

Introduction

1

HUMILITY AND LEADERSHIP

Why So Many People Are Calling for It Today

> A leader is always first in line during times of criticism and last in line during times of recognition.
>
> *Orrin Woodward, founder of Amway*

Find the Humble Leader

Let's start by asking maybe the toughest non-rhetorical question in the entire book here at the beginning. Which of the following leaders would you consider to be humble? Jesus, Kim Jong-il (the late supreme leader of North Korea), Tony Hayward (former BP CEO), John Wooden (the late UCLA basketball coach), Margaret Thatcher (the late former British Prime Minister), Mahatma Gandhi (leader of the Indian independence movement). Do you think everyone could agree that even one of these people is humble? We doubt it and our doubt is not borne from cynicism, but from experience. We've been researching humility for nearly a decade. Over that time, we've found that people can make a case that just about anyone who ever lived wasn't always humble. We've come to accept this fact and continue writing about humility in leadership because it's a fascinating topic and the inclusion of humility in the discourse on leadership has great potential for making a difference in the lives of organizational leaders.

Demonstrating Humility

Humility is expressed through action. It is something someone does. Yet, it begins with one's thinking. People demonstrate humility in their interactions with others when they have perspective about themselves, their roles in relationships with others, and their place in the larger scheme of things. It can come through in one's dealings with direct reports, with clients, with friends and family, and even with the grocery store clerk. Not everybody has or acts with humility and that's fine. Even people who demonstrate humility don't always behave with it in every situation. As you read through the chapters you will see that we cover humility from a lot of different angles and while many of those describe humility as a quality, humility ultimately comes through as a behavior.

Who We Have Written This Book for

More so now than ever, people are writing and talking about humility. What is it? What does it mean to be humble? Is humility a good thing to have or to show? Are leaders more effective with humility? As the world grows more connected and people are exposed to different cultures and ideologies, people are experiencing and experimenting with different ways of leading. Leading with humility is one of the most intriguing, albeit somewhat counterintuitive, forms of leadership being embraced. To help guide and nurture the discussion, we have written *Leading with Humility*.

We have written this book for people who are intrigued by humility, but don't understand it and really don't understand what it looks like when it comes to leading. This book is for aspiring leaders, leaders who still think they have room to grow, and for leadership scholars. And while this book provides for a more thorough understanding of humility, how it is enacted, and suggestions for how to cultivate it in individuals, the conversation regarding humility and leadership is in its infancy. Much more will be revealed as leaders recognize the role humility has in leadership and academics continue to build the body of research on humility and leadership. The basic text of *Alcoholics Anonymous* (1976) said it best: "Our book is meant to be suggestive only. We realize we know only a little" (p. 164). So let's make it clear right now that we often fall far short of integrating humility into our daily lives and we're not here to convert anyone into a humility zealot or to tell you it's the one best way for you to lead. But, if you are currently a leader or plan on becoming a leader and want to know more about what humility is and how one can lead effectively with it, you have found the right book.

Related Emerging Theories and Writings on Leaders

Our book complements and, we hope, advances current scholarly and managerial thinking on leadership. Over the years, researchers have explored leadership with very different lenses. In most recent years, however, there has been strong focus on creating or developing positive leadership theories. Some of these emerging theories and studies conceptually lend support to the notion that humility is a desirable leadership quality, and they are gaining a lot of steam. Jim Collins (2001), for example, is credited with introducing the importance of leader humility in popular management literature, sparking more interest in theories such as authentic leadership and servant leadership in the scholarly circles of universities as well as in the managerial ranks of "real" organizations. Gaining the attention and respect of both PhDs and CEOs is no small feat.

So we think it's worth spending some time highlighting this work right at the onset. We'll briefly introduce you to four emerging theories below: level 5 leaders, authentic leadership, servant leadership, and spiritual leadership. Each, in its own way, demonstrates the importance of a different kind of leadership than has been promulgated in the past—leaders who strive to see a "bigger" picture for the long term, be true to themselves, and positively relate to others.

Level 5 Leaders

In his bestselling book, *Good to Great*, and related articles, Collins (2001) researched over 1,400 of the largest companies and found that only 11 achieved exceptional financial performance for 15 years after a major time of change. These 11 companies each had a level 5 leader. Collins' levels each describe a different type of effective leader, with the first level capturing highly capable individuals with good working habits. Level 5 leaders blend professional resolve with personal humility. The humility of a level 5 leader manifests itself by the leader acting quietly, calmly, and determinedly. When successful, level 5 leaders give credit to others, the environment, and luck—as opposed to themselves. However, they shoulder the blame when the company fails to meet expectations. Collins is less sure that Level 5 leadership can be developed and suggests that some have a level 5 seed while others don't.

Authentic Leadership

Authentic leadership has recently received much attention from practitioners and academics. Authentic leaders are consistent in leading from their values and are genuine in their relationships with others (George, 2003; Yukl, 2013). In his book on the topic of authentic leadership, the highly regarded former CEO of Medtronic, William George (2003), describes the five key dimensions of authentic leadership: purpose, values, relationships, self-discipline, and heart. He prescribes authentic leadership as the antidote to the celebrity CEO. Research has found that employee perceptions of authentic leadership are a strong predictor of employee job satisfaction, organizational commitment, and workplace happiness (Jensen & Luthans, 2006). Authentic leadership is also positively related to follower performance (Hannah, Avolio, & Walumbwa, 2010, as cited in Avolio & Mhatre, 2012) and predicts organizational citizenship behaviors (i.e., actions outside of an employee's job description that benefit the organization) (Walumbwa, Avolio, Gardner, Wernsing, & Peterson, 2008).

LEVEL 5 HIERARCHY

FIGURE 1.1 Jim Collins' *Good to Great* level 5 hierarchy
Source: Good to Great. Copyright © 2001 by Jim Collins. Reprinted with permission from Jim Collins.

Servant Leadership

Robert K. Greenleaf retired from AT&T as the director of management research in 1964. Six years later, he published an article, "The Servant as Leader" (reproduced in Greenleaf, 1991). Servant leadership theory proposes that servant leaders have a duty to meet the needs of others first and their primary purpose is to help followers grow. Greenleaf distinguished between people who are servants first versus those who are leaders first. According to Greenleaf (1991), the choice to serve first aspires one to lead. These leaders put the interests of followers ahead of their own (Bass & Bass, 2008). These types of leaders also take a holistic approach to work, promote a sense of community among followers, and share power in decision making responsibilities (Spears, 1996). They are service oriented and directed by what their organization and followers need. Despite its intuitive appeal, there is less empirical research on servant leadership theory than on many other leadership theories. However, the existing research suggests that for followers, servant leadership strengthens goals related to growth, pursuing ideals, and seeking opportunities to achieve aspirations. Servant leadership is also positively related to team effectiveness (van Dierendonck, 2011). Interestingly, several measurement instruments that have been developed to identify servant leadership indicate that humility is a key component (van Dierendonck, 2011).

Spiritual Leadership

Finally, spiritual leadership is another theory that has recently picked-up in research interest from academics. Fry (2003) suggests that spiritual leaders create a vision for members of an organization to experience a sense of calling in that their life has meaning and makes a difference. Spiritual leaders also establish an organizational culture of altruistic love in which leaders and followers demonstrate care, concern, and appreciation for themselves and others (Fry, 2003). Research on spiritual leadership has found a significant positive correlation between employee life satisfaction, organizational commitment, productivity, and sales growth (Fry, 2003). More broadly, the concept of leading with spiritual based values has been researched and findings have suggested that the values can increase commitment, teamwork, sense of service, and personal growth (Milliman & Neck, 1994, as cited in Bass & Bass, 2008). In developing the theory, Fry (2003) suggested that spiritual leaders demonstrate humility by being of service to others.

What these emerging theories tell us is that people may want something different from their leaders than what the media and others promote as celebrity leadership. Leadership has a profound amount of influence on the world and in the development of others. These theories have recently flourished because people recognize how important good leaders are to the community. The increasingly diverse workforce and various stakeholders are demanding a new kind of leadership, one in which leaders relate to their followers. People want more from their leaders. They want leaders who care about their employees—both in terms of their development and their work product. They want leaders who care about the community and demonstrate it by reinvesting in the community. They want leaders who realize they have a responsibility to the future—in terms of sustainable business practices and eliminating waste. We believe leading with humility may be one way that leaders can achieve such positive influence.

Section and Chapter Overview

Part I: Our introduction sets the context needed for readers eager to explore leading with humility. The goal in the opening of this chapter was to get you thinking about humility and how challenging it is to associate humility with a specific person. We also sought to introduce you to several emerging leadership theories that suggest the need for new models of leadership.

These recent theories suggest the field of leadership research is growing and argue for the importance of morally upstanding leaders who support followers rather than solely focusing on maximizing the leader's own output. In Chapter 2, "Rethinking (Your) Leadership," we encourage readers to rethink traditional notions of leadership and to begin reflecting on their own leadership and humility.

In Chapter 3, the first chapter of Part II, we define humility. In the process, we cover humility's historical and etymological roots. We also juxtapose dictionary definitions of humility with definitions that are developing from academic research on the subject. Chapter 4 covers the first of three components that make up the definition of humility: Understanding yourself. In this chapter, we discuss self-awareness and the importance of understanding one's strengths and weaknesses. We also provide an overview of some of the most well-known biases that threaten self-awareness. Chapter 5 discusses the second component of humility, relating to others. There we describe different identity orientations and unpack the specific levels through which we relate to one another: cognition, affect, and behavior. The third and final main component of humility, perspective, is described in Chapter 6 where we dive deeply into the concept of perspective taking and outline its importance in exercising humility. We also discuss the developmental stages of perspective taking that evolve over one's lifetime.

In Part III of the book, we focus on practical applications of humility for leaders. Chapter 7, "Everyday Leadership," offers five behaviors for leaders to act more humbly and discusses what it means to have followers attribute humility to leaders. "Why Humility Matters: Empowering Followers" is the eighth chapter and there we discuss how leading with humility may uniquely empower followers and why this is important. Chapter 9 adds to the application section by encouraging readers to cultivate humble leadership and provides several concrete exercises that leaders can start practicing immediately. Finally, in Chapter 10, we conclude by calling on all leaders to embark on their journey toward humble leadership despite the obstacles that might arise.

As this first chapter comes to a close, keep in mind that this book is largely academic in nature. Although we certainly expect you will grow from reading it, it's not a self-help book, or a "how to" course, and it doesn't have a ten step action plan to transform your life. However, over the course of the chapters that follow we ask you often to reflect on difficult questions regarding leadership and humility. We define humility and delve deeply into each one of its core components. We talk about how humility is applied in everyday leadership situations and with followers. Interspersed throughout the book, there are case studies of different leaders who have demonstrated humility at various points in their life. The Appendix also includes an assessment tool for evaluating humility. Overall, our goal is to provide an in-depth and, at the same time, accessible look at what it means to lead with humility.

Closing Thoughts

Emerging (and increasingly popular) theories of leadership such as authentic, servant, and level 5 leadership suggest that people are interested in understanding more about humility. However, very few authors have attempted to articulate what humility means and why it is so important to good leadership. Our aim in writing this book is to make the connection between humility and leadership clearer. Let's begin by questioning traditional notions of leadership and reflecting on how you practice leadership.

2

RETHINKING (YOUR) LEADERSHIP

There is nothing noble in being superior to your fellow man; true nobility is being superior to your former self.

Ernest Hemingway, author and journalist

Overview

Before the book delves into the research regarding humility and leadership, we believe it is important for you to take the opportunity to reflect on your thoughts about leadership and leading with humility. This chapter will ask you to rethink traditional notions of leadership, reflect on your own leadership style and your ideas about humility, and consider the importance of empowering followers, advancing shared goals, and leading for a common good. The reason for this is simple: research has shown that leaders who develop inspiring visions with followers produce long-lasting and sustainable results (Yukl, Seifert, & Chavez, 2008; Yukl, 2006). This requires considerable time and effort on the part of the leader. Leadership—whether enacted with short-term or long-term impact in mind, for the betterment or not of followers, or to advance the personal goals of the leader or the collective good of a community—is, at the end of the day, still very hard work. If leading for the short term or long term both require considerable efforts, then why not choose to exert that effort toward leading in a manner that ultimately produces sustainable and impactful results? Why not choose to lead in a way that listens to and advances the interests of the collective, that seeks to achieve a common good for all involved rather than pushing ahead individual or even organizational interests?

One reason is simply because many leaders do not yet know *how* to lead in this way. Organizational training on leadership, when made available, frequently focuses its content on more traditional (and even outdated) notions of leadership. Poor training coupled with the pressures of organizational life that focus one's attention on predetermined goals that must be achieved within tight timeframes, can make it surprisingly difficult to lead toward a common good. Yet, many leaders do it, and they do it well. One of the most iconic and successful CEOs of recent decades, Jim Sinegal, for example, is well known (and in some circles on Wall Street, infamously well known) for the unapologetic manner in which he supports his Costco employees with benefits and treatment above industry norms. During the times when pressures were highest, Jim responded not by changing his leadership approach, but by doing what was necessary to sustain it through the down periods, such as holding his salary steady at $350,000 a year from 1999 to his retirement in 2011, while relying on company stockholdings to increase his net worth. His total compensation in 2010 was $3.5 million, which is significantly higher than the average employee's, but paltry compared to his peer group's median: $9.3 million (McGregor, 2011). Just like Jim, other leaders who lead toward shared goals and the betterment of others can't imagine doing it any other way. How did they get there? While the paths are many, we suspect that at some point (likely many points), they simply sat down and thought deeply about what leadership is—its power, its promise, and its responsibility to the followers being led.

Throughout this chapter we provide you with space to begin your internal dialogue about important leadership questions. We'll ask you to reflect and collect your thoughts on questions such as these: How do you lead? How did becoming a leader change you and your behavior toward others? How do you currently define humility? What does it mean to lead with humility? As a leader, how are you treating your followers? First, let's rethink the traditional notions of leadership a bit further.

Rethinking Traditional Notions of Leadership

Myth: Effective Leadership Is Strong Leadership

Many traditional notions of leadership conjure up ideas of people with larger than life personalities, who are supremely confident and influential. They are classic "alphas," whose outgoing personality and strong conviction in their beliefs take command of a room and don't let go. They are in charge and there is no doubt about it. Even though the idea that a certain set of traits makes someone a powerful leader has been challenged by researchers for decades (e.g., Stogdill, 1948), effective leaders are often portrayed in the popular media as outgoing, ambitious, confident commanders (Collins, 2001). These types of people enter with such a presence and conviction that others are influenced to their way of thinking. If you have thought this description represents an archetype of leadership, this book is going to challenge you to revisit what it means to be a leader.

Myth: Leading for the Common Good Doesn't Work in Organizational Settings

Leading for the common good is anything but easy. Public leaders who make leading for the common good their raison d'être face skepticism and challenges from the media and others. Business leaders who espouse striving toward the common good seem especially suspect and are faced with myriad questions: for example, can a company claim it is concerned about the depletion of natural resources when it consumes huge quantities of resources as a part of its daily business operations? Do large companies show concern about the common good when their entrance into communities often results in the displacement of smaller businesses and, arguably, negative impacts on the local economy? Can leading for the common good occur when publically traded organizations are pressured to deliver strong stockholder returns quarterly?

For top organizational leaders, focusing on the common good alongside, or even instead of, focusing on their organization's immediate success is not an easy chore. Even for the best leaders, focusing on the common good can be seen as an aspiration that is far too lofty for for-profit firms. Yet, CEOs of publicly traded companies are now more than ever struggling to establish goals such as building communities and making their own employees healthier rather than solely focusing on growing the organizations they oversee, building market share, and increasing stockholder returns. The leaders of many privately held companies face a similar situation, and a similar desire to meet multiple goals that impact their organization as well as their communities. Even leaders of not-for-profit organizations can get so focused on their organizations' objectives (including how to sustain their existence) that they lose focus on the bigger picture. Yes, those who really want to lead for the common good have many obstacles to overcome.

As "The Tragedy of the Commons" (Hardin, 1968) suggests, people will often attempt to maximize their own returns. Garrett Hardin's influential essay from 1968 illustrated that an individual acting in self-interest to maximize his own benefit often does more harm than good. The lack of consideration for others and for the future can inadvertently negatively impact the greater good by depleting resources. Even for the most successful leaders, the potential for disconnect between self-interest and the common good is hard to eliminate. However, such leaders are able to find shared values and focus the group on accomplishing goals that greatly benefit the common good. By taking a perspective that considers how to benefit communities and by developing a vision for the organization with followers, organizational leaders who lead for the common good enable themselves and others to transcend self-interests, and even the interests of their organizations. This does not mean that organizational or self-interests cannot be aligned with community interests.

Your Turn: How Do You Lead?

Now that we've begun to share with you some of the recent notions of leadership that have emerged from our research, we ask you to reflect upon your leadership style. Stop for a moment and ask yourself: How do I lead? Really ask yourself. Say it out loud if you are feeling courageous. "I lead by ..." In describing how you lead, you are saying something about yourself. You are taking a position about what you value and how you think things should happen. Don't worry about this humility thing quite yet, but really pause, reflect, and think this through. Take it a step further by grabbing something to write with and jotting down your response on the inside cover of this book so it's easy to find when you want to reference it later. So go ahead, take a moment, and ask yourself: How do I lead?

Reflecting on your leadership, both as enacted and as desired, is important. This is because each of us comes to the table with experiences of leading and being led and we also bring the baggage of our bad leadership-related experiences and our stereotypes about leadership. Your understanding of leadership has been greatly shaped by your bosses, parents, peers, government officials, mentors, and so on. And remember, your followers' understanding of leadership has been shaped by their own prior experiences as well.

Our experience in the classroom with hundreds of undergraduate and graduate business students has shown us that people differ widely in their ideals for leadership. Some think the most effective way to engage followers is to ooze charisma, be suave, and have those followers in the palm of the leader's hand. Others think a much more dictatorial approach will produce the best returns by keeping a close eye on followers and having them compete against each other. Still others will argue that every situation is different and therefore calls for the leader to be flexible; sometimes they need to be a drill sergeant, other times they need to be more akin to a statesman. Whichever approach you take, it sends a message to your followers. For you to be a successful leader, it is important that you have a clear understanding of how your followers are interpreting the message you are delivering.

Have You Changed Now That You Are a Leader?

While it intuitively makes sense leaders will be good at taking another's perspective, some research has found the opposite by looking at the effects of power. Galinsky and his colleagues (Galinsky, Magee, Inesi, & Gruenfeld, 2006) undertook a series of experiments that primed undergraduates with different states of power (low and high and a control group) and then had the undergraduates draw an E on their own forehead. Some of them drew the E in a self-oriented direction (backwards for someone looking at the E) while others drew it in a direction that was outward facing. They found that feelings of power resulted in drawing the

E in a self-oriented direction thereby demonstrating less perspective taking, less interest in others' emotional states, and a lower understanding of how others understand the world around them. In another extensive series of experiments, Galinsky and his colleagues (Galinsky, Magee, Gruenfeld, Whitson, & Liljenquist, 2008) found that feeling powerful greatly reduces subtle situation pressures to conform in comparison with people who were primed to feel less powerful and with those who were not primed at all. Think about that and its implications. For better or for worse, when people feel powerful, they are less thoughtful toward others. These interesting findings on power can be extended to leadership and our point is we behave differently in different leadership situations.

What Does It Mean to Lead With Humility?

Earlier we asked you to describe your leadership style. Now ask yourself: How would you change if you were to lead with more humility? We suggest that a necessary first step to leading with humility is to articulate your own definition of humility. What is humility? Again, we encourage you to jot down your answers. With respect to defining humility, try not to over-think it at first. Capturing your initial thoughts and impressions provides an important window for understanding your true beliefs and attributions about humility. Now that you have recorded your answers, we'll ask a few more tough questions. Would leading with humility bring you to be more self-aware in your speech and behavior? Would you be more in tune with followers? Would you have a better understanding of the bigger picture? Leaders with humility are not saints. However, they have a better idea of what's happening in terms of their own actions, their relationships with followers, and the bigger picture than those without humility. If you lead with humility would you be better than you already are at leading for the common good?

How Do You Treat Your Followers?

As a final area for self-reflection in this chapter, let's segue into a discussion of the leader's relationship with his/her followers. A leader who is in touch with his/her followers recognizes how well followers understand and support the organization's desired goals. Further, the leader understands what followers expect and need from the leader and from peers to help the followers embrace organizational goals. Effective leaders understand that followers' needs will differ according to the experiences and attributes of the follower. Additionally, leaders that focus on the common good, in addition to defining a beneficial end state, are keenly aware of the motivations and goals of followers. A leader's job is the synergistic work of aligning organizational and individual goals. So, how do you treat your followers when you are leading them?

Unfortunately, many leaders don't understand the importance of evaluating themselves, not only on their progression up the career ladder, but also on their ability to ensure the welfare of followers and the welfare of the organization. After all, they may have made it into their position of leadership because of their seniority or past performance. Regardless of how or why the leader got there, his/her followers will know how in tune the leader is with them. Being out of touch manifests itself in followers not feeling supported or not feeling listened to and feeling a disconnect between their goals and those of the organization.

Our point is that how leaders treat others matters a lot. Followers and others pick up on the subtle and not so subtle ways leaders treat them. As such, leaders, whether they are new to leadership or have decades of experience, should take the time to think about common myths and assumptions about leadership and see how it matches up with what their followers need from a leader.

Concluding Thoughts

In sum, this chapter's combination of rethinking traditional notions of leadership, asking yourself about how you lead, and considering the message you send to followers is designed to help you reflect on your leadership style. Then, by asking you to consider the meaning and role of humility in leadership, we hoped to bring a new lens to your previous leadership experiences. As we've outlined above, there are several aspects of traditional notions of leadership that we argue require revisiting, such as the necessity for great leaders to be strong personalities and a broadening of organizational leadership responsibility toward leading for a common good.

With these new views of leadership as the backdrop, we define humility in Chapter 3.

CASE STUDY: LEADERSHIP, HUMILITY, AND POPULAR CULTURE

Where Do Our Notions of Humility and Leadership Come From?

Many of us grew up watching television—even if we were only allowed an hour a day, a few hours a week. According to a recent study, 70% of American youth between the ages of 8 and 18 have televisions in their rooms (Uzoma, 2011). School age children watch about 4.5 hours of television per day on various devices (including telephones). The potential for popular culture to influence our understanding of leadership and humility is enormous. So, what messages are we likely to receive?

Reality television shows such as *Survivor* offer one view of leadership—the most competitive and politically savvy person is the leader . . . and the winner. According to a 2001 *Psychology Today* article (Reiss & Wiltz, 2001), one of the commonalities of many popular reality shows is competition. The article's authors, Steven Reiss and James Wiltz, conducted a survey to better understand the characteristics of reality show watchers and found that viewers tended to be competitive and place a high value on revenge. As a result, such shows may reinforce skewed views of leadership among a population who already sees life as a cutthroat competition.

Yet, all pop culture versions of leadership are not so malevolent. A number of movies have portrayed views of leadership that contrast with the notion that leaders are the strongest, the most competitive, and the most manipulative. An American classic, *It's a Wonderful Life*, demonstrates a different kind of leadership. George Bailey, a long-suffering, small town business man is a local leader, albeit unwillingly. His leadership takes the form of caring for others, engaging in self-sacrifice, and taking on unscrupulous business leaders. A particular telling scene is when customers of the local Building and Loan, of which George Bailey is president, make a run on the bank during the Great Depression. George's speech provides an excellent demonstration of leading by invoking people to care for one another. Here is what he says:

> You're thinking of this place all wrong. As if I had the money back in a safe. The money's not here. Your money's in Joe's house . . . right next to yours. And in the Kennedy house, and Mrs. Macklin's house, and a hundred others. Why, you're lending them the money to build, and then, they're going to pay it back to you as best they can. Now what are you going to do? Foreclose on them? . . . Now wait . . . now listen . . . now listen to me. I beg of you not to do this thing. If Potter [owner of the town bank] gets hold of this Building and Loan there'll never be another decent house built in this town. He's already got charge of the bank. He's got the bus line. He's got the department stores. And now he's after us. Why?
>
> Well, it's very simple. Because we're cutting in on his business, that's why. And because he wants to keep you living in his slums and paying the kind of rent he decides. Joe, you lived in one of his houses, didn't you? Well, have you forgotten? Have you forgotten what he charged you for that broken-down shack? Here, Ed. You know, you remember last year when things weren't going so well, and you couldn't make your payments. You didn't lose your house, did you? Do you think Potter would have let you keep it? Can't you understand what's happening here? Don't you see what's happening? Potter isn't selling. Potter's buying! And why? Because we're panicky and he's not. That's why. He's picking up some bargains. Now, we can get through this thing all right. We've got to stick together, though. We've got to have faith in each other.
>
> *(Capra, 1946)*

In this pop culture film, one of the most famous of all time, George Bailey reminds us that the person who leads, who exerts influence in times when people might turn against one another, is not the person who tricks them or beats them back with sticks. Instead, the leader is the person who asks them to remember their obligations to each other and their collective vision.

For your consideration, we offer the following questions:

- How has pop culture influenced your view of leadership?
- What characters in movies or fiction demonstrate leadership?
- What behaviors cause you to label the character(s) as a leader(s)?

PART II

Humility

3

HUMILITY

The Definition

I have three precious things which I hold fast and prize. The first is gentleness; the second is frugality; the third is humility, which keeps me from putting myself before others. Be gentle and you can be bold; be frugal and you can be liberal; avoid putting yourself before others and you can become a leader among men.

Lao Tzu, philosopher

Why Define Humility?

Without a precise and usable definition, it is surprisingly hard to identify humility. Indeed, we often think of humility in terms of the absence, rather than the presence, of particular qualities. For example, when humility is absent, most of us can readily and easily cite arrogant behavior. However, we have trouble identifying when people are engaging in humility. The difficulty in defining humility is, in part, due to the lack of rigorous analysis of the concept over the years. As a result, the word signals different meanings for different people and this makes it a confusing concept with myriad and sometimes conflicting definitions. Moreover, we would argue that too often humility is infrequently acknowledged, misidentified, or altogether overlooked. Yet, perhaps the most common problem associated with defining humility is that people mistakenly equate humility with weakness and modesty—concepts we will demonstrate later are quite different than true humility.

Examples of the absence of humility are widespread and rampant today. Long-running American television shows, such as *The Apprentice*, play up the behavior of leaders belittling others. Indeed, there are even bestselling books about leaders with big egos and larger-than-life personalities. Donald Trump (Trump & Schwartz, 1987) provides a fitting example with his bestseller, *Trump: The Art of the*

Deal. "The Donald" is an example of a leader who is pushy and acts strong. He tends to play up his strengths and rarely acknowledges his weaknesses, at least publicly. If benefits happen to accrue for the community, so much the better, but it's clear that he is focused on benefitting his own self-interests. Former Fortune 500 CEO Bill George's book on authentic leadership calls out the problem with celebrity CEOs: "In large measure, making heroes out of celebrity CEOs is at the heart of the crisis in corporate leadership" (George, 2003, p. 11). Like Trump, most of these larger-than-life leaders seem to have little use for humility. In terms of media consumption, the spectacle of grandiosity seems to always capture more interest and attention than humility.

Yet, despite the notoriety that comes from the popular press's superstars, many people *are* interested in humility. While they may be highly entertained by Donald Trump's infamous "You're fired!" many do not want him as *their* boss nor do they wish their boss to act like *that*. Humility is also a popular topic in certain aspects of leadership and in religious studies. However, the lack of clarity over how humility is defined and what humility looks like in real life prevents the concept from creating much meaningful dialogue. Despite the dearth of examples, there have been a few extremely successful presentations of humility, which suggests the importance of the topic.

A case in point is Jim Collins' (2001) book, *Good to Great*, which has been translated into 29 different languages and was listed for six years on *Business Week*'s bestsellers list. As discussed in our first chapter, *Good to Great* brought the notion of level 5 leaders to the mainstream. These leaders transform their organizations from merely good organizations to great performers. They create that transformation through a combination of humility and professional will. Will, according to Collins, is to deliberately choose a course of action. That sense of resolve and determination is easy for most to spot. Interestingly, Collins' important work provides little in the way of a definition when it comes to the topic of humility, noting simply that level 5 leaders credit others, external factors, and luck for the organization's success while shouldering all of the blame when the company does not live up to expectations (Collins, 2001). Certainly, humility is a challenging concept to recognize and seems even harder to define. As such, our next section explores humility's recent past to help inform the definition.

Recent work by academic researchers has begun to shed some light on the definition as humility has become a more popular research topic. Part of the reason for this popularity has to do with the advent of positive psychology. Positive psychology is a burgeoning field within psychology for academics and practitioners alike who are interested in building positive qualities at the individual and collective levels. For decades psychology's primary focus in studying the mind has been to treat illness. In contrast, the mission of the field of positive psychology is to understand and develop the strengths and virtues that help people and communities to flourish (University of Pennsylvania, n.d.). Positive psychology looks at strengths, virtues, and values. Included among these positive qualities, is humility. At the 1998 annual meeting of the world's largest association of psychologists, the American Psychological Association, the theme of the year was positive psychology (Wallis, 2005). This brought credibility and mainstream attention to this field of study. Since then interest in the topic and growth of this subfield of psychology have exploded with dozens of published books, hundreds of scholarly articles, conferences, and even a Center for Positive Psychology at the University of Pennsylvania.

The Origin, History, and Etymology of Humility

Humility's origins come from the Latin word *humilitas*, which can be translated into the English word "humus." Humus is the organic matter that remains after animals and vegetables decompose. When humus goes into the ground, it provides nutrients that enable new life to grow. As such, it is the most fundamental component of the life cycle. It has been compacted over thousands and thousands of years to provide a starting point for other life that comes out of the dirt. It is literally part of the earth. It makes sense then that humility is sometimes equated with lowliness. However, humility's etymological roots, by their description of humility's generative facets, also provide an understanding of why humility has a much richer connotation. The essence of new life is the result of vegetables and other matter breaking down and this makes humus the key ingredient in the regenerative process. It is apparent that humility's roots have deeply shaped how we understand the earth in its most fundamental states. Humility's connection to the earth is much less well known than humility's connection to religion.

Historically, many references to humility came from religious and philosophical teachings. The Catholic Church's Catechism identifies humility as one of the seven virtues, and Catholic candidates for sainthood are judged by those virtues (Woodward & Miller, 1994). Not surprisingly, most of the modern day academic references to humility include a religious context (e.g., Morris, Brotheridge, & Urbanski, 2005; Owens & Hekman, 2012). Philosophers have also explored humility, especially Kant. Kantian philosophers have defined humility as "that meta-attitude which constitutes the moral agent's proper perspective on herself as a dependent and corrupt but capable and dignified rational agent," (Grenberg, 2005, p. 133) and suggested that it is seminal to other virtues (e.g., forgiveness, courage, wisdom, and compassion) (Owens & Hekman, 2012).

Defining Humility

Over the course of our research, we looked across a diverse field of opinions to better understand how humility is conceptualized. What we came to see was a gap between the popular culture and dictionary definitions of humility and the way researchers and scholars describe humility. This gap is developing into an "old way" and a "new way" of conceptualizing humility (Lawrence, 2008). For example, the fourth edition of *The American Heritage Dictionary* defines humility as "the quality or condition of being humble" and defines humble as "1. Meek or modest. 2. Deferentially respectful. 3. Low in rank or station" (Pickett, 2001, p. 415). Many dictionaries focus on humility as a modest or unassuming quality associated with lowliness and share *The American Heritage Dictionary*'s description of humility. Despite some degree of consensus among word experts, we have found from a variety of sources, including informal conversation, religious teachings, scientific research, and even studies of larger groups of people, that many understand humility to be a much richer construct than dictionary definitions suggest.

Based on our research, we define humility as a personal quality reflecting the willingness to understand the self (identities, strengths, limitations) combined with perspective in the self's relationships with others (Nielsen, Marrone, & Slay, 2010). Embedded within this definition are three key components integral to humility— understanding yourself, relating to others, and perspective—which are outlined below. This definition builds on previous definitions and conceptualizations of humility (e.g. Exline & Geyer, 2004; Morris, Brotheridge, & Urbanski, 2005; Ryan, 1983; Tangney, 2000; 2002).

Core Components

In following chapters, we extensively cover each of humility's core components, so we will simply outline them here:

- *Understanding yourself*—Developing self-awareness of your strengths as well as your weaknesses.
- *Relating to others*—Seeing yourself in terms of your relationships and being as concerned about the welfare of others as you are about your own welfare.
- *Perspective*—Experiencing oneself and life events in relation to a greater whole.

What Humility *Is*: A Virtue

Humility is a virtue. Virtues are positive aspects of our character. Moreover, they are learned and can be developed and honed over time. While virtues are generally thought of as beneficial qualities, what is defined as a virtue depends

TABLE 3.1 Defining humility: There's an old way and a new way

Old way	New way
Meek	Self-aware, including strengths and weaknesses
Modest	Open
Unassuming	Low in self-focus
Deferential	Others orientated
Lowliness	Perspective
Virtue	Virtue

very much on who is being asked. For Plato, virtue came about from channeling one's thoughts and actions into benefits for the individual and society. Aristotle believed virtue resulted from life experiences that came about from the balance of two extreme characteristics (McCullough & Snyder, 2000). McCullough and Snyder cite an example in which self-control was the resulting virtue of balance between indecisiveness and impulsiveness. They define virtues as thoughts, reasons, emotions, motivations, and actions that enable a person to think and act in order to produce benefits for self and society (p. 3). Virtues, then, are qualities that enable one to have a basis for action that is intended to better society while also bettering the individual. Humility serves as such a basis for individuals; for leaders in particular, humility enables leaders to harness resources and people to achieve outcomes benefitting self and society that could only be achieved through collective action.

The book, *Character Strengths and Virtues* (*CSV*) (Peterson & Seligman, 2004), has proven to be an important work in reenergizing interest in the topic of virtues. Its editors, Peterson and Seligman, pointed out that there is no reference source to diagnose positive characteristics (what is right with people). They seized the opportunity to undertake research that resulted in a new way for the field to explore promoting wellness. They presented 24 strengths under 6 virtues: wisdom, courage, humanity, justice, temperance, and transcendence. In *CSV*, humility is classified as a character strength under the virtue of temperance. This cardinal virtue shows up consistently across cultures and throughout history. Temperance is generally understood as demonstrating restraint in thought, word, or action. Thus, it makes sense that humility is often equated with modesty.

What Humility *Is Not*: Important Distinctions between Arrogance, Modesty, and Humility

Humility is a unique construct in that it is often mistakenly defined as the opposite of arrogance or the act of being modest. While these two concepts are important, they do not provide much assistance in truly understanding humility. Imagine being described as the "exact opposite" of your sister or "kind of like" your brother. Not only are those comparisons unhelpful, they miss the fundamental distinction that you are you and that no one else—sibling or otherwise—is quite like you. If humility was somebody's sibling, then it would be understandable if humility had a complex. Let's briefly consider first arrogance and then modesty.

Arrogance

Arrogance is "a stable belief of superiority and exaggerated self-importance that are manifested with excessive and presumptuous claims" (Johnson et al., 2010, p. 405) and is characterized by disparaging others in interpersonal contexts

(Silverman, Johnson, McConnell, & Carr, 2012). In a series of experiments, Hareli and Weiner (2000) found that arrogance is associated with undesirable qualities that are internal to the person, stable over time, and uncontrollable. Not surprisingly, research has found that arrogant people elicit less admiration from others than modest people do (Hareli & Weiner, 2000). The sense of supremacy that comes with arrogance is easy to spot. Nobody likes it. It's damaging to personal relationships.

When people in positions of leadership are wrapped up in arrogance, their decisions are being made in a state of delusion. The behavior of political and military leaders can epitomize this poor decision making behavior. The decision to commit a country's soldiers to war must be an agonizing one. When a president commits countrymen and women to war most would expect that all other reasonable means have been exhausted and that the war is just. When war is based on a leader's will to force and control, that is a prime example of arrogance.

Modesty

Modesty is the quality of being unassuming or having a moderate estimation of one's self (Woodcock, 2008). Researchers have found that people who behave modestly in response to their performance tend to be better liked than those who respond boastfully (Bond, Leung, & Wan, 1982). Additionally, self-presentation literature suggests that others consider demonstrations of modesty by an individual to be less threatening to the others' self-esteem (Jones & Wortman, 1973, as cited in Wosinka, Dabul, Whetsone-Dion, & Cialdini, 1996). In looking at different levels of modesty (e.g., high, moderate, and low), findings indicate managers prefer medium presentations of modesty from subordinates while co-workers prefer high demonstrations of modesty from other co-workers. Not surprisingly individuals who present in a boastful manner (i.e., low modesty) are consistently responded to more negatively than their moderately modest or highly modest counterparts (Wosinka et al. 1996).

However, just as humility is not simply the opposite of arrogance, humility is not the equivalent of modesty. Equating humility with modesty is the most common misconception of humility we have discovered in the course of our research. Revisit your notes from Chapter 2. Did you make this misconception when we asked you to define humility? When a person demonstrates modesty they underrepresent the importance of their positive traits, contributions, and expectations (Cialdini & DeNicholas, 1989). They tend to downplay the importance of an accomplishment. They don't want the person they are speaking with to overestimate the magnitude of the accomplishment. They care about not hurting the feelings of the person they are talking to more than they care about the recognition they might receive (Woodcock, 2008). As Ridge (2000) philosophized, a modest person deemphasizes his/her accomplishments and beneficial traits, does not care much about whether they are esteemed or whether they get everything they are entitled to, and somewhat cares that other people do not overestimate their accomplishments and positive characteristics.

Not for Every Leader or Every Leadership Situation

In the following chapters, we delve deep into the three core components of humility and we provide sound and actionable strategies for how to maximize the impact of your leadership with humility. Yet, are there leadership situations where it might be best to *not* demonstrate humility? Yes, we believe there are. Even for those who exude humility, there will be times when it's best not to let it shine.

We are hard pressed to find an example of when a leader doesn't benefit from possessing humility, but there are some times when it's best to not demonstrate it. For example, when a leader needs to act quickly in crisis events, it may not be best (or even feasible) to engage all of the components of humility. Instead, the leader should act to avert the crisis.

Closing Thoughts

In this chapter, we highlighted opposing viewpoints on humility. Specifically this chapter detailed the old and new ways people describe humility and we compared humility with other descriptors that are often positively and negatively related with humility (i.e., modesty and arrogance, respectively). Importantly, we also introduced our definition of humility and its three core components. The definition deserves more detail. In the next chapter, we provide that detail by looking at humility's first key component: understanding one's self.

CASE STUDY: WILL THE HUMBLE LEADER STAND?

What Is Meant by "Exercising Humility in Leadership"?

Throughout this book, we will draw on our definition of humility, but here in Chapter 3, we provide our first indepth discussion of the definition. Therefore, we'd like to solidify the concepts by providing an example of a leader and applying the concepts presented to her leadership. Tawakkol Karman was one of three women awarded the Nobel Peace Prize in 2011 for their roles in leading non-violent struggles in various parts of the world to assure equal rights for women (Tawakkol, n.d.). While Karman's work focuses on women, she says she was initially motivated to act because of injustices she saw perpetuated by the Yemeni government. Specifically, Aryn Baker and Erik Stier of *Time* report:

> She says she has protested hundreds of times, both in the country's north and the south. But it was the refusal of the government to

intervene in the case of the Ja'ashin, a group of 30 families that were expelled from their village when the land was given to a tribal leader close to the President, that launched her on the revolutionary path. "I couldn't see any sort of human rights or corruption report that could shake this regime. They never responded to one of our demands. It made it clear to me that this regime must fall."

(Baker & Stier, 2011)

This vivid imagery gives us a picture of the motivations behind Karman's leadership. She is able to consider the expulsion of 30 families as bigger than the problems of *those* families. The expulsions were really about *all* families because the regime's inhumanity could easily extend to anyone. Indeed, she is able to see that withholding rights from women is not about *just* women. There are larger issues and concerns at stake——human rights and social justice. Karman's focus and efforts suggest that demonstrating transcendence and perspective taking is an important part of exercising humility.

However, transcendence and perspective taking alone do not constitute exercising humility in leadership. Humble leaders are also aware of their strengths and weaknesses yet they are not modest. For example, Karman decided to give up wearing a veil because she felt that women involved in activism and protests needed to be seen and, as wearing the veil is a traditional practice rather than one required by Islam, she removed it. It is not hard to imagine that some might consider this an immodest act, an action that signaled her lack of humility. We would not say so. Nor could we agree that the act of removing the veil was arrogant, it was simply an attempt to communicate better and lead more effectively.

Finally, Karman is a relational leader. She has demonstrated her willingness to sacrifice and march in the street with her followers. A report from Assia Boundaoui of *The World* (2011) shares the following:

Althaibain [a follower] said Karman has proved herself time and time again. Althaibani recalls one particular demonstration in Sana'a. "I get a call saying Tawakul is leading the march, and the youth are behind them and we're running there and then we hear shots," Althaibani said. She said Karman was taken to a makeshift hospital, and then came right back.

In such dangerous situations, leaders of movements are often whisked away because they are seen as too important to remain in the context where they might be hurt. However, Karman attends to her injuries and returns to the scene of the protest, demonstrating her solidarity with the protestors.

For your consideration, we offer the following questions:

- Based on our definition, Tawakkol Karman appears to be a humble leader. What do you think?
- What information influences your thinking on this question?
- What other information might be helpful?

4

UNDERSTANDING YOURSELF

You cannot be a leader, and ask other people to follow you, unless you know how to follow, too.

Sam Rayburn, former speaker of the US House of Representatives

Vipassana: Seeing Things as They Really Are

A lot of people find it hard to really be in the present and who can blame them? They are busy thinking about the past or the future and struggle to stay in the now. To combat this some people work out, others turn off their cell phone, and still others have developed elaborate note taking systems in order to try to put distractions out of their mind and into a physical or virtual space. Then there are the people who silently meditate … for 10 consecutive days, in a meditational practice called Vipassana. Vipassana is an ancient Pali word meaning to see things as they really are. It is one of the oldest forms of sitting meditation with an overarching goal of eradicating human suffering (Vipassana meditation, n.d.).

Participants wake up at 4:00 am and meditate until 9:30 pm with three small food breaks in between. Those who meditate in Vipassana show an increase in self-acceptance, and overall positive effects on one's self-concept (Emavardhana & Tori, 1997). We would also surmise that they are quite a committed group of people who are striving to know themselves. In working toward seeing things for what they really are, the retreat participants also get to understand themselves for who they really are. Like practitioners of Vipassana, leaders exercising humility strive to know themselves and see things as they are so that they can effect change.

Leading with humility requires leaders to be able to look at themselves reflexively and from the standpoint of others. As a result, they understand how others see them and have an understanding of who they are apart from others' viewpoints. For example, they may incorporate how others see them into their understanding and make adjustments when appropriate. In contrast, they may seek to help people understand them as they understand themselves (Swann, Stein-Seroussi, & Giesler, 1992). Throughout this chapter, we offer a deeper look into this self-understanding component of humility by defining and discussing self-awareness as well as threats to and facilitators of self-awareness. Let's begin with a definition of self-awareness.

The Relationship between Self-Awareness and Leading with Humility

Self-awareness is defined as the "ability to assess others' evaluations of the self and to incorporate those assessments into one's self-evaluation" (Atwater & Yammarino, 1992, p. 143). Self-awareness begins a process of self-evaluation. In this process, the "real" self is measured against an ideal self. For example, let's say that you look at your face in the mirror and see a blemish on your cheek and dry skin under your lower lip. Before looking in the mirror, you were unaware of the blemish or patch of dry skin. The differences between the real and ideal self in this example lead to dissatisfaction. To ease the dissatisfaction, you might try applying cover-up cream to diminish the blemish or moisturizer to get rid of the patch of dry skin. Alternatively, you could decide that you're fine with the blemish as it is. In either case, having looked in the mirror allows you to understand how others will see you as you move through the world. Similarly, when individuals become more self-aware by looking into the "mirror" provided by others, they can react to their reflection by attempting to mitigate the dissatisfaction (Duval & Wicklund, 1972) or decide they are satisfied with their reflection. For leaders with humility, it is important for them to understand how and why people are reacting to them the way that they are.

What's a Strength? What's a Weakness?

Many of us define strengths and weaknesses as those *skills* at which we excel or fail. However, some authors define strengths as personal talents, natural abilities, or "continuing and recurring patterns of thought, feeling or behavior" (Asplund, Lopez, Hodges, & Harter, 2009, p. 6) that are magnified when we are in situations that align with our passions, "satisfactions" (Buckingham & Clifton, 2001, p. 75), and values (and are diminished when in situations where such alignment is lacking). Buckingham and Clifton go on to define strengths as "consistent near perfect performance in an area" (Buckingham & Clifton, 2001, p. 25). In contrast, weaknesses are defined as "anything that gets in the way of excellent performance" (Buckingham & Clifton, 2001, p. 148). Weaknesses may include skill deficiencies but are not limited to such deficiencies. A weakness may also be a framework or mindset that gets in the way of outstanding performance.

We feel it is important to emphasize clear definitions of strengths and weaknesses because doing so may help leaders to acknowledge, discuss, and appropriately deal with weakness as they seek to become more humble leaders. For example, imagine you are an accountant and you don't know how to balance a ledger. Of course, being unable to balance a ledger is a skill deficiency, which gets in the way of outstanding performance and may be improved by training. Therefore, it is a weakness (one that is easily remedied). However, without clear definitions of strength and weakness, leaders might never move past skill deficiencies and consider that weaknesses may also be frameworks or mindsets that impede performance and prevent leading with humility.

A Word of Caution about Strengths

Although natural talents are strengths, we suggest some caution in thinking that a natural ability *always* equates to a strength. Indeed, there are times when people have natural ability and yet have little interest in engaging in a skill area. We argue that when people are deenergized by performing a strength they will have little interest or inclination to invest in it and, over time, their strength will diminish. Therefore you may learn about your strengths and weakenesses by discovering when you are energized about your "work" and by examining those activities you consistently perform well.

How Do You Know If Your Strengths and Weaknesses Really Are *Your* Strengths and Weaknesses?

As you try to assess your strengths and weaknesses, let us point out that we do not think you have to *agree* with others' perceptions of your self to have good self-awareness. Rather, good self-awareness means you have an understanding of how others perceive you. Moreover, we argue that critically examining others' perceptions is extremely important for leaders who may be members of stigmatized groups (e.g., women, minorities). The perceptions of members of these groups may be marred by stereotypes and prejudice. Therefore, imbibing poisonous views of oneself would not be equivalent to building an accurate view of self. Yet, confronting stereotypes and prejudice may be the first step to productive engagement in difficult conversations that result in more positive working relationships (Ely, Meyerson, & Davidson, 2006). At other times, you may agree with the perceptions of others and then be able to use their perceptions to improve your leadership.

The Responsibility of Self-Awareness for Leaders Exercising Humility

Self-awareness also helps one better understand and ultimately be in touch with one's moral convictions. As Gibbons (1990) surmises, the self-focused person is concerned about what action is most appropriate and what should be done in a given situation. If there is no self-focus in a situation requiring a moral stance, the individual's behavior may be driven by the needs of the environment or habit (Gibbons, 1990). In being fully self-aware, an individual is able to identify the personal rules they have decided are worth following. These moral rules help to govern behavior.

Is being self-aware alone sufficient to lead with humility? No. Leading with humility requires self-awareness, relating to others, and transcendence or perspective. Indeed, we argue that leaders who exercise humility have a special need to focus on self-awareness because they are attempting to lead people to outcomes that are not just important for the leader or for an individual team member (or even perhaps for all team members). To illustrate this concept, let's consider college basketball coaches. Fewer than 1.5% of the best NCAA division I college men basketball players go on to play at the professional level (NCAA, 2012). Therefore, college basketball coaches are also expected to be mentors and guidance counselors to their players. Some would argue that their vision must extend beyond winning the next game or making it to the postseason. Coaches are often encouraged and expected to build the character of their players and help them prepare for life after an athletics-focused college career. Therefore, the coaches who are exercising humility will desire to understand how they are perceived because they have a vision beyond winning; they are focused on a transcendent vision (transcendence will be discussed further in Chapter 6). A basketball coach exhibiting humility in leadership is cognizant of how their behavior influences winning *and* character building.

Finally, leaders exercising humility know that self-awareness brings an element of vulnerability. Once you know your strengths and weaknesses, you are obligated to act on them in some way. If you now see that there is an area that is impeding performance, you must address the deficiency either by gaining the necessary skills, challenging an existing framework, or expressing your need for others to fill in the gap in your own knowledge or skill base. Similarly, now that you are aware of your strengths, you must bring them to bear on the problems at hand. You can no longer stand on the sidelines. Being self-aware challenges us to act based on our strengths and weaknesses.

Summing Up

In conclusion, leaders who exercise humility are aware of themselves and how they are viewed by others. Leaders that are self-aware are not subservient to the perceptions of others but they are not oblivious to them either. They use the information they gather from others to inform their understanding of their strengths and weaknesses and this knowledge becomes important in effectively leading others.

Threats to Self-Awareness

While leaders exercising humility strive to be self-aware, there are some important threats to self-awareness that we would like to mention. These are narcissism, neuroticism, cognitive biases, and heuristic biases, as they present serious challenges to the exercise of humble leadership.

Narcissism and Narcissistic Personality Disorder

Of course, there are many different forms that a lack of awareness or inaccurate self-awareness can take, but since this book is about leadership and humility, we felt narcissism warranted special attention. For psychologists and other doctors, the *Diagnostic and Statistical Manual of Mental Disorders* (*DSM-IV*) (American Psychiatric Association, 1994) is the handbook and reference guide to under-standing, classifying, and defining disorders. Narcissistic Personality Disorder (NPD) is a diagnosable condition in the *DSM-IV* (1994). NPD is a "pervasive pattern of grandiosity, need for admiration, and lack of empathy" (American Psychiatric Association, 1994, p. 658). According to the *DSM-IV* (1994), people afflicted with NPD have an inflated sense of self-importance, are preoccupied with imagining themselves as powerful, beautiful, loved, and successful. Individuals with NPD genuinely believe that they are superior and expect others to recognize this superiority. They require excessive admiration. They expect favorable treatment. They exploit others. They lack empathy. At the same time, they become jealous of others or believe that others are jealous of them. They are often patronizing or rude. To qualify as a disorder, these patterns need to be stable over time and situations. Also (sorry parents of teenagers), it doesn't qualify as a disorder if it's understood as a normal part of a developmental stage.

Neuroticism

Feelings of anxiety and fear form the basis of neuroticism. It is also related to an overall negative mental state and can include depression, self-consciousness, impulsiveness, and vulnerability (Saulsman & Page, 2004). In personality tests, high neuroticism scores are related to a lack of self-confidence and self-esteem (Judge & Bono, 2000; McCrae & Costa, 1991). Thus, intuitively it makes sense that neuroticism and leadership would be negatively related. However, Judge and Bono (2000) did not find support for a hypothesized negative relationship bet-ween neuroticism and transformational leadership. Moreover, additional research by them and their colleagues (Judge, Bono, Ilies, & Gerhardt, 2002) concluded that neuroticism "failed to emerge as a significant predictor of leadership" (p. 774). Therefore, neuroticism and leadership are certainly not mutually exclusive and people who tend toward neuroticism can also be leaders.

Cognitive Biases

Cognitive biases result when the logic an individual uses to draw conclusions or adopt beliefs is flawed (Haselton, Nettle, & Andrews, 2005). For example, people tend to ignore research evidence because it doesn't match their life experience. Simply put, biases happen. Sometimes biases are detrimental, sometimes they are beneficial, and sometimes they don't matter whatsoever. However, people who understand themselves are aware that they regularly operate with biases.

Moreover, the extent of our bias is surprising; research has uncovered numerous cognitive biases inherent to our human brain and these biases are extremely influential on how we think and make decisions (Bazerman & Moore, 2008). In this section, we focus particularly on a subset of these—heuristics—because of their importance in understanding ourselves as well as the large degree of research confirming their influence across a variety of situations faced in our everyday lives. Interested readers can look to other books such as Max Bazerman and Don Moore's (2008) *Judgment in Managerial Decision Making* for detailed discussions of other biases.

Heuristic Biases

The word "heuristic" is defined as an educational method of learning through investigation and discovery (Pickett, 2001). Heuristic biases are judgment shortcuts to facilitate decision making (Shedler & Manis, 1986). Humans use shortcuts in making decisions all the time. It's commonsense. Commonsense, however, is an example of a heuristic bias. After all, having all of the information for why something is the way it is could overwhelm us and certainly isn't needed in most instances. The mind therefore creates simplified shortcuts to help us process all of the data we consume. Take, for instance, the common example of a job interview. If a prospective employee is interviewing for a job at a start-up tech company and the prospective employee comes in wearing a formal and traditional business suit, the interviewer may be using a heuristic bias to disqualify the candidate before he/she says a word. The employer may be thinking that the candidate isn't a good cultural fit based solely on appearances because current employees never wear suits into the office. Regardless of how qualified and personable the interviewee is, the interviewer is engaging a heuristic bias to disqualify the candidate.

Availability Heuristic

Credited to Tversky and Kahneman (1973), the availability heuristic is when decisions are too heavily based on readily available information. Events in which examples are prominent or easily retrievable influence the perceived probability of the event occurring. This is one way the mind makes determinations. For example, if all of the case studies in a book highlighted women CEOs as leading with humility, those reading the book might overestimate the number of women CEOs who lead with humility. This heuristic can certainly be helpful; however, with it, people are more likely to overestimate the likelihood of improbable events.

Representative Heuristic

Basing the probability of an event on what's familiar is another common bias called the representative heuristic. That is, people predict by representativeness when they select or order outcomes based on the degree to which the outcomes represent important features of the evidence that a person has (Kahneman & Tversky, 1973). Below is a brief example.

Mark is a leader, confident, an excellent communicator, and describes his vision to others effectively. His emphasis on empowerment and goal setting is lauded by his colleagues. Is Mark more likely to be a CEO or a K–12 teacher? Since there are many more male K–12 teachers than there are CEOs, Mark is more likely to be a teacher. However, the descriptors we use for Mark are often representative of how one would describe a CEO rather than an elementary school teacher.

In sum, leaders exercising humility make themselves conscious of their cognitive biases and understand the positive and negative roles of heuristics when they make decisions. They do this so that they can better understand themselves. They know that understanding who they are allows them to understand how they lead. And understanding how they lead is perhaps the most crucial element to leading effectively.

Closing Thoughts

Mom was right when she told you to just be yourself. There is a difference between pushing yourself to grow, or challenging yourself to improve, and trying to act like someone else. The former leads to improvement while the latter comes across to others as inauthentic. From a leadership perspective, this is an important distinction. No one wants to follow a leader who comes across as inauthentic. The successful balance comes from still being you while introducing the managerial and leadership aspect of your position into your interactions with followers. Bridging that gap allows followers to see you for the leader you really are, not the leader you think you should be.

Leaders with humility are deeply self-aware and actively work to understand who they are, their strengths and weaknesses, and how others see them. As such, it becomes next to impossible to leave behind their authentic self in leadership situations. Remember however, that while understanding the "self" is a critical piece of humility, it is not the whole. It is one of three highly intertwined components comprising humility. In our next two chapters, we discuss relating to others and perspective taking.

CASE STUDY: SELF-AWARE NOT SELF-EFFACING

How Do Leaders Exercising Humility Exhibit Self-Awareness without Becoming Effete?

Chapter 4 discusses the importance of leaders having a sound understanding of strengths and weaknesses and behaving with authenticity. To illustrate our conception of leaderly self-awareness, we present William George, an extraordinary businessman who took Medtronic from $755 million in sales to $5.5 billion in 12 years between 1989 and 2001 (George, 2007). However, George is also well known for his emphasis on the purpose of business and authentic leadership.

He talks about the importance of corporations being mission driven, value centered, and possessing an adaptable business strategy (van de Ven, 2001). But perhaps what most attracted us to him was his awareness of strengths and weaknesses. He shares the following:

> I ran for office in my college fraternity six times and lost every time . . . at this point a group of seniors took me under their wing and gave me some sound advice. "Bill, you have a lot of ability, but you come across as more interested in getting ahead than you are in helping other people. No wonder no one wants to follow your lead." Although devastated by this feedback, I took their advice to heart. I talked to my peers about what I was doing wrong and how I could change.
>
> *(George, 2007, p. 60)*

As he matured, he recognized the importance of surrounding himself with people who are "more knowledgeable and experienced" than he was (George, 2007). As an illustration of this principle, George shares a story about his early tenure at Litton Microwave Cooking Products. The story begins during the early days of microwave oven usage when the Food and Drug Administration (FDA) announced that cooking with the appliance might be hazardous to a person's health. As you can imagine, this announcement negatively impacted sales. George knew that creating a strategy to deal with the FDA and create a product that was safe was critical. So, what did he do?

I was not an expert in any aspect of the business, yet in this crisis everyone looked to me for survival . . . I survived the crisis only by forming a team with my subordinates, relying on their superior expertise, and prodding them to work together. My skill was to pull together the right people and empower them to solve the problems, one at a time. This is a pattern I have followed throughout my career, as I have lacked substantial industry experience in every leadership job I've had.

(George, 2003, p. 93)

We call your attention to this example because we think it is important to pause and reflect on the last sentence. George recognizes his strength— pulling the right people together and enabling their success. And, he readily admits that he has often lacked industry experience. However, he does not castigate himself for not being an industry expert. On the contrary, George is able to see the key to his success as being self-aware and then behaving in alignment with self-knowledge. Perhaps our favorite George quote is:

For years I felt I had to be perfect, or at least appear that I was on top of everything. I tried to hide my weaknesses from others, fearing they would reject me if they knew who I really was. Eventually, I realized that they could see my weaknesses more clearly than I could. In attempting to cover things up, I was only fooling myself.

(George, 2003, p. 15)

Bill George is a leader who understands that while he has weaknesses, he also has strengths. Understanding these weaknesses and making allowances for them is essential to leading well. To do otherwise is to plan to fail. Therefore, he acts interdependently (forming teams to solve problems) but always recognizes that he is the leader and must act with courage and conviction. At times, this may cause him to go against the advice of colleagues or employees. Yet, such actions are always taken after careful thought and consultation. For your consideration, we offer the following questions:

- How does the humble leader exhibit self-awareness (especially knowledge of weaknesses) without becoming effete?
- Are you acting in concert with your knowledge of your strengths and weaknesses?

5

RELATING TO OTHERS

Leaders must be close enough to relate to others, but far enough ahead to motivate them.

John Maxwell, author, speaker, and pastor

Crisis Clinic: Relating to Others in Need

Every day over 250 people call the not-for-profit Crisis Clinic in Seattle. At this phone line, volunteers are able to field calls only after an extensive 60 hour training regimen. The program is so highly regarded in the region that some of the local police department's hostage negotiation teams are required to take the training. Each crisis line caller is in some sort of emotional distress. One of the callers may be the mother of a son who took his own life and she is calling on the anniversary of the suicide. Another may be really angry because his girlfriend just broke up with him. Some are simply having a bad day. Ups and downs are a part of life and it's nice to know that you are not alone. So when you call the crisis line, someone answers and they listen to you. They don't tell you what to do or where you should go. They don't tell you that they know how you're feeling even if they have been in a similar situation. They simply listen and demonstrate care and empathy.

Humility involves relating deeply to others. Those with humility focus on their interdependence with—rather than their independence from—others. Said another way, they think of themselves in terms of their relationships to others. As humility scholar June Tangney (2000) suggests, a central part of humility is an "others" orientation. When you operate with this orientation—as Crisis Clinic's volunteers do—it results in a powerful motivation to advance the welfare of others and to better the communities to which you belong.

This second component of humility is a complex one. Relating to others involves seeing the world (and yourself) through another person's eyes. It entails validating another's feelings even when you don't feel the same way, sympathizing with others when you feel their joys and their sorrows, and drawing upon your relationships with others as you lead and as you follow. It means not focusing on yourself at times, but not forgetting about yourself as a key part of the relationship either. In this chapter, we discuss the various ways in which one can relate to others, for example through displays of empathy and sympathy, and we uncover some surprising examples of how leaders and followers are naturally drawn to relate to one another and the impact of doing so.

How you relate to others is comprised of how you think about yourself and others, how you feel about others, and how you behave toward others. Thus, this chapter discusses three fundamental levels through which a leader with humility relates to others: cognitively, affectively, and behaviorally. On the cognitive level, how a leader thinks about others is likely to be through a lens of relational identity or collective identity. How a leader with humility feels toward others (i.e., the affective level) will be discussed in part by describing empathy and sympathy. Finally, this chapter discusses how a leader with humility behaves by providing an example of the founding and continued success of one of the greatest social movements of the 20th Century, Alcoholics Anonymous.

The Cognitive Level: How You Think about Yourself in Relationship to Others

Into our discussion of relating to others, we'd like to interject two concepts explored by social psychologists—relational and collective identity orientation. According to Francis Flynn (2005) of Stanford University, understanding identity orientations enables greater understanding of why people may engage in pro-social or helping behaviors within organizations. We extend Flynn's assertions by suggesting that identity orientations may also help leaders understand how to engage people in collective problem solving aimed at transcendent visions. According to Flynn (2005), identity orientations reflect how people define themselves and answer three questions:

- What is my basis of self-evaluation?
- What is my frame of reference for self-evaluation?
- What goals or motives are present?

Let's solidify our understanding by using examples to illustrate relational and collective identity orientations. When an individual adopts a relational identity orientation, they evaluate themselves based on their adherence to behaviors prescribed by their role. Consider two faculty members in a university: Wei and Tracey. Their roles as colleagues in the university call them to support one another in research and teaching. Therefore, if Wei adopts a relational orientation, she will evaluate herself based on how well she is supporting Tracey's research and teaching. The basis used for self-evaluation is "role-appropriate behaviors" (Flynn, 2005, p. 738) and her frame of reference is her adherence to role behaviors. Finally, Wei's goal is her self-interest and the welfare of her colleague. At the end of the day, she views her self-interests as linked to Tracey's interests.

Similarly, when one adopts a collective orientation, self-esteem is linked to the "embodiment" (Flynn, 2005, p. 738) of group characteristics, and group comparisons are used to gain information for self-evaluation. For example, as a faculty member at Seattle University (SU), I may compare SU with non-Jesuit organizations that are not focused on whole person development or social justice. Therefore, my goal is to promote the success of SU faculty and SU as an institution. Flynn's research suggests that in such a case, I may be motivated to promote SU's interest at the expense of my own—at least temporarily—because of my belief in the aims of the SU community. My expectation is that I will reap societal benefits by creating "leaders for a just and humane world" (Seattle University, n.d.).

The Affective Level: How You Feel about Others

Empathy

Think about how important it is to understand the emotional states of other human beings from a social and moral standpoint. Most social interactions require at least some degree of understanding of the emotional state of another. The traditional dictionary definition of empathy describes it as the identification and understanding of another's situation, feelings, and motives (e.g., Pickett, 2001). However, empathy is much more complex. The ability to empathize with another person is one of the most fundamental ways to communicate with others and demonstrate understanding of another's emotional state. Extensive analysis of empathy by researchers who have studied how the brain handles thoughts, feelings, and behaviors (known as social-cognitive neuroscience) has shown that the concept of empathy consists of four key components (Decety & Moriguchi, 2007; Gerdes, Segal, & Lietz, 2010):

- *Affective sharing* (Decety & Moriguchi, 2007)—Affective sharing comes about when one perceives another's emotion and in doing so mirrors that emotion back. You may have noticed that you and some of your colleagues do this with each other. The next time you're talking with someone, keep an eye out for whether they start mirroring your expressions.
- *Self-awareness* (Decety & Moriguchi, 2007)—Although we have defined self-awareness in the previous chapter as an awareness of strengths and

weaknesses as seen through the eyes of others, Decety and Moriguchi use their neuropsychology lens to describe self-awareness as the ability to be the object of one's own attention. Thus, self-awareness allows one to maintain a boundary between oneself and the person receiving the empathy—despite affective sharing. Self-awareness helps people remain cognizant of their own thoughts and feelings.

- *Mental flexibility* (Decety & Moriguchi, 2007)—Mental flexibility is the ability to take the perspective of another by imagining how the other would experience the situation. We discuss perspective taking more in Chapter 6.
- *Emotion regulation* (Decety & Moriguchi, 2007)—Emotional regulation is the ability to modulate one's own feelings so that one can be effective in being empathic instead of letting one's feelings determine how one responds to another person. For example, an individual might feel frustrated in a given situation. However, the person chooses not to react on the basis of their frustration and instead chooses to react empathically or with a different emotion. Emotion regulation enables people to relate to one another without necessarily allowing a given emotion to take over. Empathizing is a powerful way to relate to others. "I see how frustrating this is for you" is an example of relating through empathy with another.

Sympathy

"I can feel your pain" epitomizes the refrain of someone who is demonstrating sympathy. Sympathy is an expression of concern or sorrow toward events in another person's life (Clark, 2010). If you ever jumped out of your seat with the heebie-jeebies from hearing a catheter-insertion-gone-bad story, you were probably sympathizing.

Empathy and Sympathy from a Leadership Perspective

Empathy and sympathy are sometimes confused by leaders. Empathy requires a leader to bring a deep level of understanding to the relationship with the follower. Leaders who demonstrate empathy are exploring a follower's situation from multiple perspectives—including the follower's and their own. When being sympathetic to followers, a leader typically experiences and conveys unison with the follower's perspective. Sympathy can include a certain presumption that the leader's experience is equivalent to that of the follower, yet in doing so, the leader can gain insight into the follower's world by feeling what he/she feels. Both types of responses can be valuable for the relationship between leaders and followers.

The Behavior Level: How You Behave toward Others

A powerful example of what can happen when individuals relate to one another can be found in *Time* magazine's list of the 100 most important people of the 20th Century. Bill Wilson (Bill W.) is the co-founder of Alcoholics Anonymous and a member of *Time's* august group. Not surprisingly, some describe Bill W. and co-founder Dr. Bob Smith (Dr. Bob) as humble leaders. They created a self-help program that thrived like no other in modern history and the program itself often discusses humility. In fact, according to AA's second most published text, the *Twelve Steps and Twelve Traditions* (Alcoholics Anonymous, 1981, p. 70), the attainment of greater humility is described as the foundation principle of each of AA's 12 steps. One of the reasons we think the co-founders of AA were humble was because of the way they structured the organization and specifically the way AA meetings were conducted, which created a safe space for people to be listened to. In an AA meeting, a recovering alcoholic shares while the other recovering alcoholics listen attentively. The listeners discover ways they can relate to the speaker. Because AA members see their self-interests (i.e., getting sober) as tied to this process of caring for others in their quest to be sober, the care they take in listening and being there for one another is an excellent example of relational identity. Bill W. and Dr. Bob knew that one person relating to another would play an important part in helping people stay sober.

The Story of Alcoholics Anonymous: Relating to Others through Shared Situations

At its core, Alcoholics Anonymous describes itself as a fellowship where members can share their experience, strength, and hope with each other in order to recover from alcoholism (Alcoholics Anonymous, 1976). Thousands of AA meetings are held around the world every day. In these meetings, people sit together and listen to each other share. Each person typically introduces himself by saying, "My name is _____ and I'm an alcoholic." Then that person goes on to share about either a topic that has been presented or whatever is on their mind. When the person is finished sharing, the other members collectively say "Thanks ____." AA, through its declaration of Traditions, has worked hard to minimize its organizational structure and avoids taking positions as to why things happen the way they do in order to allow the individual groups to have autonomy to fit the needs of the group's members. Notice in Figure 5.1 that an AA group's collective membership is at the core of its structure. Service positions such as public information representative, secretary, and chairperson are important, but the leadership and decision making ability resides within each respective AA group, not the service positions.

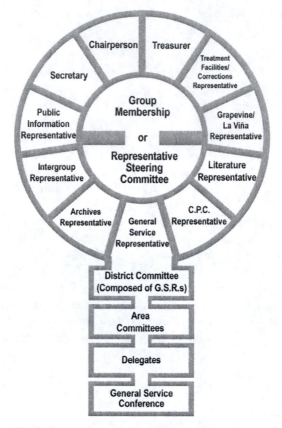

FIGURE 5.1 The Alcoholics Anonymous Service Structure

Source: The "Service Structure Inside The A.A. Group" chart is reprinted with permission of Alcoholics Anonymous World Services, Inc.

It is clear that one of the primary reasons AA meetings convene is because they provide AA members with a place to relate to others who are experiencing or have experienced many of the same feelings and situations that are being shared. Thus, part of the way people recover from alcoholism is by sharing with each other and relating to what others are sharing. The reciprocity in this process reaffirms for recovering alcoholics that they can live through experiences and feelings without having to drink. The affirmative head nods in an AA meeting and collective laughter that suggests others can relate to what is being shared helps others and the sharer heal. AA is sometimes referred to by its members as a healing community. This description seems quite fitting as there is no other program quite like 12 step meetings that enable one to get better, in part, by relating to others. As AA compellingly demonstrates, even from its very beginnings, relating to others is an important component of humility.

AA Co-founder Bill Wilson

AA came into being because a New York stock broker, Bill Wilson, was visiting Akron, Ohio on a business trip and happened to be staying in the Mayflower Hotel in May of 1935 (Alcoholics Anonymous, 1980). Wilson was freshly sober for the umpteenth time and trying to stay that way. It was not an easy commitment to hold on to and Wilson was not enjoying himself. While standing in the hotel lobby, he could hear laughter from the bar and feel the warmth and comfort that some hard alcohol would provide a stranger from out of town. He paced up and down Mayflower's lobby, before finally having the notion that if there was any chance of him staying sober, that chance would come from him working with another alcoholic. In the 1930s, hotels had phone directories with names and contact info of local ministers. Wilson found the Mayflower's minister's directory and started calling. The first reverend who answered gave Wilson 10 names to call. The first nine calls Wilson made were to people who either couldn't help or didn't answer. The tenth and last person on the list, who answered, Henrietta Sieberling, must have been caught at least a little off guard when she heard Wilson introduce himself as a "Rum hound from New York" (Alcoholics Anonymous, 1980). The term, alcoholic, was not widely used then. He continued by telling her that he had found a way to stay sober and needed to share it with another "drunk" if he were to have any chance of staying sober himself. Sieberling said she did know someone who she thought could greatly use his help and would go about setting up a get together.

AA Co-founder Bob Smith

At about the same time Bill Wilson was asking operators to connect his calls from the Mayflower, physician Bob Smith was laying in his bed trying to sober up (Alcoholics Anonymous, 1980). He had walked into his kitchen earlier that day, carrying a Mother's Day plant for his wife, when he collapsed drunk on the floor. He was helped upstairs by his wife and school aged children and ordered to rest in bed. Smith was in his mid-50s and alcoholism had taken its toll on his once promising career. He was a surgeon at Akron's City Hospital and formerly regarded as one of the area's finest surgeons, that was until the heavy drinking that had started in medical school 20 years prior could not be kept hidden from his colleagues. They had lost a tremendous amount of respect for the doctor.

Bill and Bob Meet

Henrietta Sieberling was friends with the Smiths and after talking with Bill, she called Bob's wife, Anne, to talk about the possibility of setting up a meeting between Bill and Bob (Alcoholics Anonymous, 1980). They scheduled a dinner for the next evening. When they all arrived that next day, Dr. Bob told Bill that it was nice to meet him, but thereafter Bob wanted no part of the dinner and announced that he needed to leave. Bill responded by making a quip about Bob being thirsty and from there the conversation continued for several hours. That night, when one alcoholic sat down and talked with another alcoholic about staying sober, is credited with being the beginnings of Alcoholics Anonymous.

However, addiction to alcohol is not an easy thing to be rid of and while Bill had taken his last drink, Bob got drunk once more before sobering up for the last time in June 1935. He went on to help hundreds of people directly and millions of people indirectly. Dr. Bob was a straight shooter: "I don't believe I have any right to get cocky about getting sober. It's only through God's grace that I did it. I can feel very thankful that I was privileged to do it" (Alcoholics Anonymous, 1980, p. 222). When Bob first met a prospective new member of Alcoholics Anonymous, he often presented the program of AA on a take it or leave it basis. If he heard someone share at a meeting and he thought they were being dishonest, he would pull that person aside and tell him so. He also demonstrated a relational identity by being quick to remind fellow sober alcoholics that being of service to other alcoholics was a favor to themselves in helping to ensure their own sobriety.

Relating through Tolerance

Certainly Dr. Bob could be described as direct; most accounts of Dr. Bob suggest that he was curious, open to new ideas, and willing to change. He also related to others through tolerance. In AA's magazine, the *Grapevine*, Dr. Bob wrote about tolerance:

> During nine years in AA, I have observed that those who follow the Alcoholics Anonymous program with the greatest earnestness and zeal not only maintain sobriety but often acquire finer characteristics and attitudes as well. One of these is tolerance. Tolerance expresses itself in a variety of ways: in kindness and consideration toward the man or woman who is just beginning the march along the spiritual path; in the understanding of those who perhaps have been less fortunate in education advantages; and in sympathy toward those whose religious ideals may seem to be at great variance with our own. [. . .] Tolerance furnishes, as a by-product, a greater freedom from the tendency to cling to preconceived ideas and stubbornly adhered-to opinions. In other words, it often promotes an open-mindedness that is vastly important—is, in fact, a prerequisite to the successful termination of any line of search, whether it be scientific or spiritual. These, then, are a few of the reasons why an attempt to acquire tolerance should be made by each one of us.
>
> *(as quoted in Alcoholics Anonymous, 1980, p. 273)*

Relating through Communication

Communication is a way in which leaders relate to others. The medium through which the communication occurs can take various forms, but it all starts with communication. For instance, Bill W. and Dr. Bob were insistent about not using their full names in AA meetings and in more public forums regarding the program. They led by communicating their values. Leaders with humility are also inquisitive. They want to know why. They want to know how. They want to know about others and how choices will impact others. They ask clarifying questions to ensure they and others adequately understand the situation. They do this so that they can be intentional and effective in communicating their concern for others and their recognition of another's experience and perspective, even when making decisions that followers may not like. They also ask probing questions. When a humble leader asks a probing question, they are getting others and themselves to think deeper about the topic at hand. Writing, pats on the back, nodding affirmations, even laughter can be used by any leader to relate to others; for those leading with humility, these are expressions of connection and consideration for the other. All of these examples of communicating are proactive. Humble leaders are not afraid to initiate and drive communication, but their approach, rooted in an "others orientation," is very different from other aggressive leaders.

Both Bill W. and Dr. Bob demonstrated humility in their leadership and managed to successfully imbue it into fellowship of AA. They worked together and with many others to create the 12 step program. As much of the AA literature attests, AA is about one alcoholic relating with another alcoholic, sharing their experience, strength, and hope. We expect that this relational identity orientation helps members of AA look for similarities between themselves, as opposed to differences, and in doing so helps create stronger bonds among members.

We also surmise that Bill W., Dr. Bob, and other members also had a sense of how important a collective identity orientation is in helping the organization to grow and flourish. Bill W. penned the original 12 Traditions to unify AA and its members (Wilson, 1983). In working to protect that collective identity, Wilson proposed in Traditions 10, 11, and 12 that AA groups should never take an opinion on matters outside of AA, that AA members should be anonymous in media, and that anonymity has an important spiritual significance for AA members, respectively (Wilson, 1983). Wilson's Traditions suggest that he and other members of AA thought it was important to emphasize that AA groups and AA members, who may have benefitted personally by publicizing their affiliation, would actually be doing a disservice to the organization as a whole. Wilson wanted to protect AA's collective identity. In particular, for Tradition 12 Wilson wrote, "It reminds us that we are to place principles before personalities; that we are actually to practice a genuine humility" (Wilson, 1983, p. 9).

Relating through Action

Sympathy, empathy, looking for similarities, communication—that's all important, but taking action is also critical to effectively relate to others. Pontificating and discussing are best balanced by working with others. Leaders make a powerful statement when they roll up their sleeves and dive in to help out in a situation. At times, the action is simply a symbolic gesture, but it's a powerful one nonetheless. By taking action, leaders speak volumes about their empathy. Ronald Heifetz and Marty Linsky write about the power of relating to followers by acknowledging loss.

> Sometimes leaders are taken out simply because they do not appreciate the sacrifice they are asking from others. To them, the change does not seem like much of a sacrifice, so they have difficulty imaging that it seems that way to others. Yet the status quo may not look so terrible to those immersed in it, and may look pretty good when compared to a future that is unknown.
> *(2002, p. 92)*

Leaders that get into action, modeling the behaviors they ask of others, provide a powerful illustration of the words that are being spoken. By modeling, leaders demonstrate that they understand the difficulty of change but also that changes must be made.

Leaders with humility take action all the way down to the front lines if necessary. They do this because humility enables the leader to see their place alongside others, within the larger community they all care about. This helps the employee have a heightened sense of ownership for their work, know that they are supported by the leader, and the leader has a better sense of what the employee is dealing with. In white collar professions, the "rolling up the sleeves" metaphor means the leader may take actions in ways such as being involved in a large sales pitch or sitting down with employees who have technical expertise in a specific area to discuss how things are going and brainstorm ideas.

Defining Yourself through Your Relationship with Others: Ubuntu

Ubuntu is a central tenet of African philosophy that reflects the belief about what is the essence of human beings. Ubuntu or "Me We" was made popular by Reverend Desmond M. Tutu during the Truth and Reconciliation Commissions hearings in South Africa in the mid-1990s (Tutu, 2007). The "Me We" philosophy encompasses who we are at a collective level as well as a relational level. The concept of Ubuntu is rooted in the belief that we are humans through our relationships with others. The essence of its meaning is captured by Tutu with phrases such as "A person is a person through other persons" or "I am a human

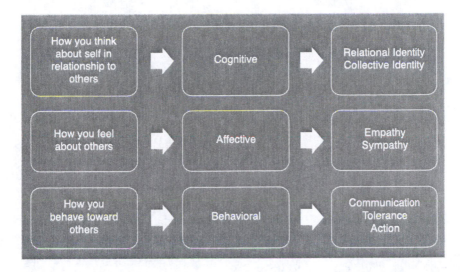

FIGURE 5.2 Relating to others

because I belong" (Tutu, 2007). As suggested by the research on collective identity orientation, our own sense of self-worth is thought to come from knowing we belong to a greater whole. We are who we are because of our connection to others. This view naturally leads to a concern for others and a tendency to be helpful and cooperative and kind. This all ties directly to the second component of humility. Those with humility are convinced of their interdependence with others. They demonstrate Ubuntu.

Beta Males: Relating to Others Can Keep You Healthy

Alpha males are a competitive group. In the wild, alpha male baboons get the best food choices and the highest number of female mates (Gesquiere, Learn, Simao, Onyango, Alberts & Altman, 2011). They wake up every day and, consciously or not, are focused on maintaining their status. After all, it feels good to be on top. They don't answer to anyone. They don't get bossed around. They get to do what they want to do. They are the kings of their social circle and dominate their beta male neighbors. They could not care less about relating to their fellow primates. However, researchers have discovered some interesting consequences of the alpha male lifestyle. Alpha male baboons experience significantly more stress than their beta male counterparts. They are compelled to protect their position by fighting other baboons who are threatening their status as a lead baboon. Alpha male baboons also spend more time following their mates to fend off passes from other males. All of these impending threats result in significantly elevated cortisol levels. Cortisol is a stress hormone. Beta males don't have anywhere near the amount of cortisol that alphas have. Nonetheless, beta males mate with almost as many females as the alpha neighbors and betas don't bother to spend nearly as much time fending off other males from their female mates.

Cortisol and Humans

Alphas in a corporate setting can be vicious: "Whenever you put alpha males together, the most aggressive will overpower the others," noted T. Byram Karasu, a New York psychiatrist who has led a CEO support group for over two decades ("Are alpha males healthy?", 2011). Alpha males are driven, competitive, and confident. However, in a group setting, one tends to emerge as the alpha of alphas. They take charge. As Karasu described, their advice to other alphas can be more geared toward establishing their own dominance within the group and lowering the others' self-esteem. Alphas thrive on adrenaline. In the corporate world, the high stress level and perceived attacks can never let up. Alpha males are very different from leaders with humility.

Leaders with humility focus on relating to others, not competing with others. They focus on "interdependence with" and not "independence from" others when making decisions. They look for the similarities they share with people. They can find a common ground. They are both sympathetic and empathetic when common ground is hard to find, yet decisions must still be made. Through it all, there is a sense of "we're all in this together" with leaders who are humble. These leaders have a sense of commitment not only to the mission and to the success of the organization, but also to the people around them.

The cortisol examples above highlight what happens when leaders are focused on competing. Their senses are heightened, but sometimes they lose sight of the goals. They focus on competition and maintaining their place in the pecking order instead of looking out into the future and focusing on how the organization can benefit its stakeholders. The costs and consequences of this approach are borne not only by the leader and his followers, but also by customers. Some might argue that the best innovation happens when leaders are focused on customers rather than on competition with colleagues.

Closing Thoughts

Relating to others is fundamental to humility. As we described at the beginning of the chapter, people can relate to each other on a cognitive level, an affective level, and a behavioral level. This chapter also explores how the founders of AA established and built the AA Fellowship on principles of members relating to other members, and on maintaining the organization's collective identity so that AA could best serve its purpose of helping alcoholics. In the next chapter, we discuss humility's third and final key component: perspective taking.

CASE STUDY: YOU WANT ME TO RELATE TO *THEM?*

How Do Leaders Exercising Humility Relate to People Who Disagree with Them?

Chapter 5 asks you to consider the ways in which leaders relate to others—usually followers, members of leaders' in-groups. While we have provided a number of examples of leaders relating to others in the chapter, it may be helpful to provide examples of people who express empathy and relate to others who are not members of the leader's in-group. That is, the "followers" are also the "enemy." What sort of behavior is used in such situations? To examine this question further, we present Nelson Mandela, a civil rights leader in South Africa who was imprisoned for 27 years for his role in the anti-apartheid movement.

As we researched Mandela, we were immediately drawn to his interest in the Afrikaners, the White minority, many of whom perpetuated apartheid. Fikele Bam, who worked with Mandela, stated:

> Nelson was very serious about learning to understand the Afrikaner—his mind and how he thought. Because in his mind, and he actually preached this, the Afrikaner was an African . . . and whatever solution there was going to be on the political issues, was going to involve Afrikaans people. They, after all, were part and parcel of the land, apart from the point that they were the rulers of the land but . . . they had grown up and they had a history in the country, which he wanted to understand. And hence he put a lot of work and effort in learning to speak Afrikaans and to use it . . . He wanted to really get to know Afrikaners, as part of the people who belonged to the country.
> *(Maharaj & Kathrada, 2006, p. 175)*

Mandela expressed empathy for the Afrikaners. He wanted to understand their perspective. He did not suggest that the only perspective worth hearing was that of Black Africans. Rather, he thought understanding Whites was equally important. Mandela's humility was also demonstrated through his habit of sharing the burdens of those who followed him. While he was a well-known political prisoner and could have traded on his own importance to secure rights or privileges for himself, he was sensitive to the welfare of all prisoners. For example, Eddie Williams, a prisoner on Robben Island at the same time as Mandela shares an especially poignant event:

> Mr. Mandela was very good to me . . . I was very sick . . . he came into my cell and comforted me and encouraged me to get better . . .

there's no waterborne sewerage . . . he gets up, puts his bucket under one arm, puts mine under the other, goes to the common toilet, empties my bucket, cleans it and brings it back. Now this man is the leader of the most powerful organization in prison. He's an international figure. He could have instructed any of his members to look after me, but he came.

(Maharaj & Kathrada, 2006, pp. 144–145)

Eddie Daniels was not even a member of the same political party. However, Mandela saw serving Daniels as important to his humanity and leadership. As always, we encourage you to ask a practical question: Does relating to people with empathy or sympathy mean that you have to capitulate to their ideals or give up your own? We argue that Mandela's life is a testament to the idea that accomplishing your vision is facilitated by understanding others. Fatima Meer, Mandela's biographer and friend, says:

I found him to be a very good, honourable and humble man, a man of great tolerance, with a remarkable capacity to see the other point of view and to come to terms with it without compromising his own ethical position . . . one can only hope and pray that he will be given the opportunity to move our country to the unity we all deserve.

(Meer, 1988, p. xixi)

The number of quotes from fellow inmates, guards, and others regarding Mandela's humility could fill a book (and have filled quite a few). Our goal is to show you a portrait of what it means to relate to others with humility.

For your consideration, we offer the following questions:

- How do leaders exercising humility relate to people who disagree with them?
- Are you exercising humility in your relationships with followers who are the "enemy"?

6

PERSPECTIVE

Leadership is not magnetic personality, that can just as well be a glib tongue. It is not "making friends and influencing people," that is flattery. Leadership is lifting a person's vision to higher sights, the raising of a person's performance to a higher standard, the building of a personality beyond its normal limitations.

Peter F. Drucker, management consultant, educator, and author

Iraq War Invasion and John Hanke: Providing a Surprising Perspective

On March 20, 2003, America's President George H. W. Bush made a prime time television address to the citizens of the United States: "On my orders, coalition forces have begun striking selected targets of military importance to undermine Saddam Hussein's ability to wage war. These are opening stages of what will be a broad and concerted campaign" (*Guardian*, 2003). The United States was dropping bombs on Baghdad and a lot of the activity was going to be picked up by media outlets.

CNN's coverage of the U.S. attack on Iraq was incessant. As a television news channel, CNN could dedicate the majority of their programming to the attack and they did. Retired military generals popped out of the woodwork to sit in from satellite news studios and discuss the implications and strategy of the attack. News correspondents phoned in live reports from Baghdad with missile blasts detonating in the background. The green haze from night vision video footage of the Iraq horizon was familiar to viewers who had watched CNN's coverage of the U.S. led Persian Gulf War in 1990. However, the way television viewers witnessed war was about to change dramatically.

Enter John Hanke, your stereotypical tech geek, who transformed how we saw the Iraq War. As a kid, he loved reading science fiction. In 2001, he started the company, Keyhole Inc., intending to build a computer generated three dimensional model of Earth. It had never been done before. John had read about such a thing in his younger years in Neal Stephenson's science fiction book *Snow Crash* (Ratliff, 2007). The results that Keyhole's developers generated took the software to the point where it was ready to be put in front of several large television studios. The studios adopted the software and waited for the right time to deploy it.

When CNN, ABC, and CBS showed simulated missile strike flights, it used Keyhole's EarthViewer maps, which could drop down to the street level in areas of Baghdad that had been shelled (Maney, 2003). It was incredible. It delivered images from decimated blast zones. Civilian viewers had never seen any technology like it before and many were fascinated by the 20 person tech company's work (Maney, 2003). Viewers were seeing images from a perspective they had never seen before. People flocked to Keyhole's website. The overwhelming response crashed the site the day after the war on Iraq started (Maney, 2003). Google was also looking at what Keyhole developed and Google's executives were impressed with the technology. So impressed, in fact, that they acquired Keyhole in 2004 and launched Google Earth a year later. What both Keyhole and Google realized was that the software provided a brand new perspective of the world. Using Google Earth, one can zoom all the way in and see the general area one lives in and then zoom back out and see the rest of the world. This new way of looking, literally, at the world has yielded some amazing discoveries and changed the way we look at things.

Perspective Defined

The American sociologist and philosopher George Herbert Mead defined perspective as "orientations within a larger context that arise through, and always remain related to, human conduct in the world" (Martin, 2006, p. 67). Put another way, perspective is one's understanding of the world that comes about from one's experiences in the world. Martin and his colleagues (Martin, Sokol, & Elfers, 2008) find that aspects of perspective include perceptual, affective, cognitive, intentional, and experiential dimensions. Thus, perspective evolves as the person evolves.

In this chapter, we take you through what it means to possess perspective in your life and as a leader. Holding perspective (i.e., considering oneself in relation to a greater whole) is the third key component of humility. We cover the complexities inherent to obtaining and utilizing perspective, and explain various thoughts on perspective, including discussions of the levels through which our ability to gain perspective grows over time and situations in which having and holding a perspective that considers oneself in relation to a greater whole is critical to leading with humility. Let's start by reviewing the five levels of perspective taking advanced by developmental psychologists.

How Social Perspective Taking Ability Grows over a Life-time

As one would expect, the ability to take perspective typically evolves over time. Developmental psychology can tell us much about how our ability to take perspective—both our own and others' perspectives—is shaped by our age and our associated stage of development. From Selman's (1980) work in particular, which is described in more detail below, we know that in young children, typically through about the age of 6, perspective is limited and involves only that which is in the immediate vicinity. However, perspective grows dramatically in children usually between the ages of 7 and 12. For instance, at some point in their development, a child begins to comprehend that others are impacted by their decisions. While the child recognizes others are impacted by their choices, a child may also think that their own thoughts represent the other person's perspective. In general, children are not yet able to see a difference between their perspective and that of others. Then, as young people, between the ages of 10 and 15, individuals are able to consider a situation from the perspective of an objective third party (despite what parents of teenagers may think).

Beginning as early as about the age of 12 and continuing on into adulthood, people are able to "abstract multiple mutual (generalized other) perspectives" (Selman, 1980, p. 40). In doing so, people taking perspective are able to realize and account for the fact that different stances toward fundamental beliefs have strengths and shortcomings. By operating with this realization, they work to develop new approaches to problem solving and to ensuring that conflicting positions are understood by all sides (Martin et al., 2008).

Selman's Five Levels of Social Perspective

To better understand how perspective taking is different from simply having an understanding of one's relationship with others, let's briefly review the levels of social perspective (Selman, 1980, pp. 37–40).

Undifferentiated Perspective Taking (Selman, 1980; ages 3 to 6)

Younger children struggle with differentiating their thoughts and feelings from the thoughts and feelings of others. They recognize that there is a difference between self and others. However, they do not understand that another may interpret a situation differently.

Differentiated Perspective Taking (Selman, 1980; ages 5 to 9)

As children grow older they realize that individuals are experiencing a feeling or emotion in a given situation, but the child believes the feeling is singular and does not understand that a person may have multiple feelings in a given situation.

Moreover, young children may believe they can understand other people by simply watching them. For example, they may think that a person who is yelling at someone is angry and the person being yelled at will be scared. They may not understand that people may yell during exciting events and the person being "yelled at" (e.g., an athlete) will not feel scared at all.

Self-Reflective Perspective Taking (Selman, 1980; ages 7 to 12)

At this stage, children understand they can take the perspective of another. They also realize that others can take their perspective. At this level, children understand that outward appearance is not necessarily inward reality. For example, they come to understand that someone may pretend to be angry or sad.

Third-Party Perspective Taking (Selman, 1980; ages 10 to 15)

This meta-perspective taking ability happens when children realize they can step out of a situation entirely and view the perspective of two parties from the stance on an impartial observer. Through coordinating these perspectives, there is a recognition of a "generalized other perspective," which, in a two way relationship, may be different for each party. So if person A and person B are in this stage and talking, both could recognize that they each have their own perspective and that those perspectives could be seen differently by outside parties. Also, it is in early adolescence that an individual starts to recognize that value systems are fairly consistent over time.

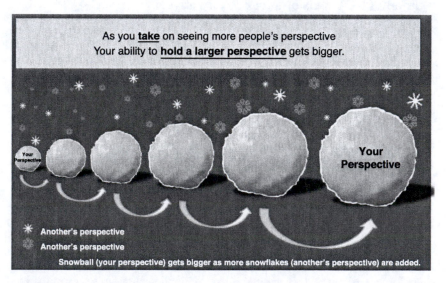

FIGURE 6.1 Perspective

Societal Perspective Taking (Selman, 1980; 12 to adult)

This last stage of perspective taking is where a person understands that while actions, thoughts, and feelings are psychologically driven, the underlying reasoning may not be understood. At this stage a person understands that their unconscious may play a role in what happens to them and this can explain why someone may do something that they do not want to do. This level is achieved when an individual understands that their ability to take the perspective of a third party can be influenced by systems of societal values (e.g., legal, moral, cultural).

Transcendence

Transcendence has been identified as a key character strength that represents a connection to the larger universe (Dahlsgaard, Peterson, & Seligman, 2005; Peterson & Seligman, 2004). Andrew Morris and his colleagues (Morris et al., 2005) reviewed the existing literature on humility and determined that transcendence "is best thought of as an acceptance of something greater than the self" (p. 1, 331), in addition to being one of humility's key components. We believe that transcendence is an important component of perspective taking. Transcendence reaches beyond the self and one's relationship with others to recognize that exchanges between people take place in a context that is infinitely greater than anyone is capable of fully understanding. As such, when a person possesses a sense of transcendence, we believe that person recognizes and appreciates that their decisions are possible because of what has come before and that decisions have the potential to impact not only what is happening today, but also may impact people in the future. People exhibiting transcendence understand that their decision can be influenced by and even influence multiple environments (e.g., ecological, spiritual, political, etc.). Put a bit more simply, transcendence happens when a person realizes that his/her decisions are a small part of a much larger universe.

While it is in the stage called "third-party perspective taking" that a person can realize that they are both an actor and object, it is not until transcendence that an individual can access the kind of consideration of other points of view we discuss as a component of humility. This means that the perspective component of humility is more than understanding another's conduct in the world. It also means that an individual has to develop a certain kind of life experience to behave with humility.

Perspective through Humility

Humility keeps accomplishments in perspective and permits interpretation of life events in relation to a broader context (Nielsen et al., 2010; Ryan, 1983). Through perspective, those with humility recognize their connection to the greater whole. They are a part of a family, a community, the world, and with that recognition they keep their talents, accomplishments, shortcomings, and failings in perspective. When something good happens, someone with humility is able to accept it for what it is. They would recognize the interdependencies required to bring about what was accomplished. Similarly, when something bad happens, it is not the end of the world. This sense of perspective enables an individual to not be strictly focused on their own needs and goals or even those of their group. Instead, they understand that they are working in a larger reality (Morris et al., 2005). As Tangney (2000) points out, people who have humility are not at the center of their own worlds. Instead, they are focused on the larger community of which they are a part.

Humility brings about a certain amount of forgetting of the self and a greater outward orientation. This is described by scholars as an "unselfved" process (Tangney, 2000, p. 72). Through perspective, one's thoughts are more focused on the external environment and others in a way that is beneficial for everyone. By not being so self-conscious, a person is able to focus on others and what's around them. This happens a lot in successful conversations. A person focused on understanding what the other person is saying, and less focused on trying to think of what to say next, is perceived to be a better listener (Kolb, Osland, & Rubin, 1995).

Perspective Taking

Walking in someone else's shoes is a colloquial way of describing perspective taking. In this instance, taking another's perspective means that one person can perceive what another person is going through. The perspective taker is looking at a situation from the standpoint of another person who is going through a specific situation. This can be a very helpful experience for both the perspective taker and the other individual. The perspective taker receives a better understanding of what might be helpful for the other person in the situation. Research has found that there are several reasons people engage in perspective taking (Gehlbach, Brinkworth, & Ming-Te, 2012):

- *When the stakes are high*—for example, when they care deeply about the other person or are threatened by the other person.
- *When the goals are altruistic*—the perspective taker wants to help the other person.
- *When situational knowledge is desired*—the perspective taker wants to better understand what's happening in a situation.
- *When building a relationship*—perspective takers are sometimes motivated to establish or improve a relationship.
- *When influence is needed*—some perspective takers are interested in influencing others.
- *When people are intrinsically interested*—a person may engage in perspective taking to better understand the person whose perspective they are taking.

- *When self-knowledge is wanted*—some perspective takers do so to better understand themselves.

Maybe it shouldn't be surprising then that individuals who engage in perspective taking tend to see themselves as possessing the stereotypic traits of the other. They think they are walking in the other's shoes. Galinsky and his colleagues (Galinsky, Wang, & Ku, 2008) found that perspective takers' behaviors actually change after perspective taking. For example, students who took the perspective of a professor performed better on a test than did a group of students who did not take the perspective of the professor. The researchers directed participants to "imagine a day in the life" (Galinsky et al., 2008, p. 406) of a stereotypic professor and a stereotypic cheerleader. Those who took the perspective of a stereotypic cheerleader scored lower on the same test. Thus, perspective taking helps people identify with and relate to others in both their thoughts and their actions. It's a beneficial quality to possess in many types of organization.

Coordinated Perspective

Coordinated perspective reflects the ability to consider multiple perspectives at the same time (Martin et al., 2008). This is analogous to a 360 degree review, but instead of evaluations made by different people, the perspective taker is thinking about the situation from numerous points of view. Perceptive executive directors take multiple perspectives into account when considering whether to add a new program to a not-for-profit's service offerings. For example, the executive director of a food bank who is considering a home delivery service would take the perspective of multiple stakeholders. How would this impact existing clients? How many new clients would benefit from this service? What would this addition mean to volunteers? Are the food bank's funders interested in supporting this potential new program? How would the food bank's board of directors perceive this change? There are a lot of different perspectives from which to explore this new service option.

How do holding perspective, coordinating perspective, and transcendence relate to one another? As suggested earlier, we all hold a certain amount of perspective. Over time, this perspective can change and hopefully grows. We expect that one of the most effective ways to extend the perspective one holds is to take multiple perspectives (i.e., coordinating perspective). When one person spends the time to think about things from multiple points of view, it intuitively makes sense that one's own perspective is enlarged as a result. Of course, this is easier said than done. Moreover, it is not certain that a person who takes another's or multiple perspectives will in fact grow from the experience. Think of a manager who tries to take an intern's perspective and mistakenly assumes that the intern doesn't have enough life experience to complete a given task effectively.

Finally, transcendence is even greater perspective. We believe that transcendence helps ground decisions because people recognize that decisions and actions have the potential to impact multiple environments and unknown stakeholders. When a person combines his/her own perspective with that of others and attempts to integrate transcendence, he/she is making an effort to recognize the multiple factors that have the potential to be impacted by their decisions.

The Importance of a Leader's Socialized Power Motive

For leaders exercising humility to take perspective in the manner required, we believe leaders needs to have a socialized power motive. Some leaders tend to exhibit personalized power motives while others demonstrate socialized power motives. What do we mean by power motives? Personalized power motives suggest that a leader is more prone to personal dominance and winning at all costs. They are not good organization builders because their followers are loyal to them rather than the organization (McClelland & Burnham, 1976). Socialized power motive leaders are driven to serve their organizations (Bass & Bass, 2008). They like the discipline of work. They willingly sacrifice self-interests for the good of the organization. They also have a strong sense of justice.

For leaders who demonstrate humility, it is essential that they look beyond their personal goals. They need to look at what is good for the organization, for stakeholders, and for the future. They also need to think beyond the organization into the community and determine how the organization's decisions will impact the community and its resources (and vice versa). Alternatively, when leaders focus on personal gains, they pay little attention to what else is happening around them. They are self-aggrandizing and willing to exploit others (House & Howell, 1992), and they are operating within the limited perspective inherent to a personalized power motive. While such leaders may be effective in some respects, they are obviously not humble.

Closing Thoughts

Imagine what it would be like to not know what we know about the Earth today. Lacking the perspective we have gained as result of science and exploration, many of us might think things like the Earth is flat, that there is an end to the Earth, that the Earth is the center of the Universe, or that the Sun rotates around the Earth. The perspective gained by scientific exploration has enriched our knowledge and our lives. Similarly, gaining perspective is a key part of exercising humble leadership. Leaders striving to be humble seek to understand that they are an integral part of a larger reality.

In this chapter, we have discussed the developmental nature of perspective, perspective taking, and when people are inclined take perspective (e.g., high stakes, altruistic goals, relationship building). Most importantly, we have discussed how taking perspective permits the enlargement of our own understanding of the world. Thus, leaders exercising humility, who engage in perspective taking, are uniquely positioned to have an expansive view of problems and their solutions.

CASE STUDY: HUMILITY, CONSISTENCY, AND PERSPECTIVE

How Does the Humble Leader Exercise Consistency without Rigidity?

We present Desmond Tutu, an excellent example of a leader who demonstrates integrity and consistency. Tutu is best known for his activism in the movement to end apartheid in South Africa, during which Tutu exhibited consistency in a number of situations.

For example, in 1985, a woman, accused of betraying the anti-apartheid movement was brutally killed by an angry mob. A week later, Tutu was asked to attend a funeral service for 14 people murdered by the South African state. While Tutu prayed for the victims of the state's actions as expected, he followed his prayer with a surprising statement. He identified himself with the crowd (using the term "we") and admonished them that the actions taken against the woman were unjust. He said:

> We have a cause that is just . . . we have a cause that is going to prevail. For goodness sake, let us not spoil it by the kind of methods that we use. And if we do this again, I must tell you that I am going to find it difficult to be able to speak up for our liberation. I will find it difficult – it is already difficult in this country to talk the truth – but if we use methods such as the ones that we saw in Duduza [where the woman accused of betraying was killed], then my friends, I am going to collect my family and leave a country that I love very deeply, a country that I love passionately.
>
> *(Tutu, 2007, p. 8)*

Tutu could not condone violence by protestors any more than he could condone the actions of an unjust regime. Both violated basic human rights. In this view, the oppressed must meet the oppressor with dignity. This perspective is one that values human rights above all else. He is consistent in his message—he does not change it because he is a member of the oppressed group. His thinking on this matter is captured in the following statement.

> Black theology has to do with whether it is possible to be black and continue to be Christian; it is to ask on whose side is God; it is to be concerned about the humanization of man, because those who ravage our humanity dehumanize themselves in the process; [it says] that the liberation of the black man is the other side of the coin of the liberation of the white man – so it is concerned with human liberation.
>
> *(Tutu, 2007, p. 16)*

Tutu is arguing that the anti-apartheid movement is not just for Blacks. It is for all people. Therefore, the principles that lead him to engage in the South African civil rights movement also demanded that he speak against violence directed at police or others who perpetuated apartheid. We assert that leaders who exercise humility live by a set of principles that guide their actions in all situations—not just some. Chief among these principles is the necessity of understanding the perspective of others and recognizing one's interdependence with, rather than independence from, others—even those who may stand in opposition to the vision. Indeed, humble leaders may welcome different perspectives more than leaders who fail to exercise humility because they see the deficits in their own perspectives and the need to garner ideas from others. In closing, we wish to share a final quote from Tutu that expresses the importance of embracing a variety of perspectives:

> It is unity we are talking about, not uniformity. What is needed is to respect one another's points of view and not to impute unworthy motives to one another or to seek to impugn the integrity of the other. Our maturity will be judged by how well we are able to agree to disagree and yet continue to love one another and to cherish one another and see the greater good of the other.
>
> *(Tutu, 2007, p. 88)*

For your consideration, we offer the following questions:

- How does the humble leader exercise consistency without rigidity?
- Are you exercising humility by taking the perspective of others—both within and outside of your team, group, organization, or nation?

PART III

Application

7

EVERYDAY LEADERSHIP

Leadership is practiced not so much in words as in attitude and in actions.
Harold S. Geneen, former president of the ITT Corporation

How Does One Behave as a Humble Leader in Everyday Life When (Often) Organizational Cultures and Societal Messages Seem to Suggest Humility Should Not Be Attempted?

Let's revisit two basic premises that we have noted previously. First, most of what we think we know about humility and leadership is wrong. Just like any other leader, humble leaders are only leaders if others allow them to express formal or informal authority to influence them (Heifetz, 1994). Therefore, the myths we outlined earlier in this book such as "humility is the same as modesty" or "humble people are weak" would lead to behavior that would be unlikely to cause people to yield the leadership role to a humble person. When people willingly cede leadership to us, it is because they see something in us that inspires them to follow our leadership. Weakness certainly doesn't inspire followership. Instead, we argue, humility inspires followers to rally behind the leader. So, what behavior demonstrates humility? Leaders demonstrate humility by listening and learning about themselves from others in order to perform better. They also exhibit humility by attending to collective and long-term interests rather than only their own concerns or short-term objectives (Nielsen, et al., 2010).

Our second premise: being seen as a humble leader matters. It isn't enough for only *you* to think you are humble. In order to execute humility in leadership, followers and others have to observe and attribute such behaviors to you as the leader. In other words, your conversation and actions must signal your humility. You must be intentional in your humility and your followers must perceive it. Ah, a seeming contradiction. How do humble leaders demonstrate their humility without losing it?

In this chapter, we provide a variety of practical tools for leaders. We address several misconceptions of humility "head on," offering five ways to behave more humbly as you lead and posing three central questions humble leaders should ask themselves daily. We also discuss three strategies for balancing humility with confidence. The chapter ends with a discussion of what happens when followers *see* their leader's humility and the very real importance of those attributions for accomplishing lasting results.

Seek to Understand Your Strengths and Weaknesses

Frances Hesselbein, President and CEO of the Leader to Leader Institute and former CEO of the Girl Scouts of the United States, provides an excellent example of effective, humble leadership and shatters many of the popular myths about humility. One common misconception is that the humble person holds him/herself in low regard (Tangney, 2002) and some will argue that the low self-esteem conception of humility will prevent one from seeing one's own strengths, as well as weaknesses. However, as we discussed in Chapter 4, humble leaders recognize their weaknesses but are also aware of and confident in their strengths (Morris et al., 2005). For example, Hesselbein is a wonderfully inclusive leader. When she was invited to apply for the CEO position of Girl Scouts USA, she considered not going because the CEO position had always been filled by someone who was serving as a leader of girls rather than in an executive position. Yet, she had a vision for scouting and when she was asked in the interview what she would do, she described a "total transformation" from an organization that was hierarchical and composed of "islands" to "One Great Movement, serving all girls of every racial and ethnic group" (Hesselbein, 2011, p. 72). She values inclusion and recognizes that one of her strengths is her ability to create and execute an inclusive vision. She is not bragging when she shares her strengths. She is simply stating facts.

Therefore, if you wish to exercise humility in leadership, you must start by having an understanding of your strengths and weaknesses. One way to do this is to return to Chapter 4 and consciously evaluate yourself. How do *you* define yourself? Are these self-perceptions accurate? How do you know? Another way to do this is by listening and seeking to understand how others perceive your strengths and weaknesses.

Now the Hard Part: *Share* Your Strengths and Weaknesses with Others

A second way to behave humbly is to share your perceptions of your strengths and weaknesses with followers. We recognize that acknowledging weaknesses is difficult for people in leadership positions. Often, people fear that voicing weakness is tantamount to providing employees, customers, and managers with ammunition to use against them in the future. Or worse, if managers are members of low status groups (e.g., stigmatized age, gender, or minority groups), then they may fear they will confirm stereotypes or appear weak or unfit for management to others. Certainly, some research would suggest that rookie managers may need to behave differently than those in higher status groups and appear more directive with subordinates (Sauer, 2011; 2012). However, we do not believe that these, or any leaders, are precluded from sharing areas of weakness with subordinates. Why? First, our definition of humility is not focused on sharing *only* weakness. We believe doing this would be a problem for any leader—experienced or inexperienced, in dominant or subordinated groups. Instead, we advocate for sharing strengths *and* weaknesses. Sharing both provides an opportunity for framing weaknesses in the larger context of the person as a whole. By doing so, one is effectively saying, "I have weaknesses" not "I am weak." This is a subtle but highly important difference. Second, our definition of humility focuses on sharing a compelling, collective vision. Therefore, subordinates will have a clearer picture of you as a leader when you share a vision and how you see the team moving toward that vision by utilizing the strengths of *everyone* present to ameliorate the weaknesses of *everyone* present—self included.

Embrace a Vision that Is Bigger than You

People often mistakenly believe that humble people are meek or display a reticence to act. Such a quality would truly be a problem for any leader. The humble leader is anything but reticent because they experience transcendence and see that there is something beyond themselves, a vision worth moving toward. As a result, they are leaders focused on serving collective interests and the needs of others (Nielsen, et al., 2010). Hesselbein states:

> Seeing and listening go together. Facing challenges, fostering community involvement, collaborating and focusing on future relevance and significance are critical for leaders *who see things whole*. These leaders put away the magnifying glass, step back from the details, and engage in the larger world. Because they engage with others and listen carefully, they see through more than one pair of eyes, using the viewpoints of others to enlarge their own perspective. Those who see the organization, the community and the society whole are the leaders of the future ... That's the big picture of listening and seeing.
>
> *(2011, p. 192; emphasis ours)*

We consider Hesselbein's statement a prescription and a challenge to those who wish to exercise humble leadership. If we are to accomplish transcendence, we must see, listen, and connect to others. What does it mean to "see"? In his groundbreaking book on diversity, Martin Davidson (2011) says that making diversity work in organizations requires people to *see* difference, rather than ignore it or pretend to be color blind in order to be politically correct.

Only when organizational members *see* difference and assume that difference matters in the work experiences of others (Davidson, 2011) can organizations leverage diversity. Similarly, we would argue that humility requires us to remove our blinders and *see* others and, in becoming cognizant of the concerns and needs of others, recognize our role in the whole. For example, Hesslbein argues for the need to "see things whole," which means that anyone who wants to understand and pursue an organization's significant priorities must see the organization as "embedded in the world at large" (Hesselbein, 2011, p. 189). They must see beyond the organization's interests and see the interests of clients, employees, customers, and other stakeholders. Hesselbein was required to model this principle when Girl Scouting had to move away from traditional scouting and consider the needs of a generation of girls growing up in a time of change (e.g., the Civil Rights Movement, Equal Rights protests). She realized that scouting had to be relevant, or as she described it "I knew that equal access, building a rich diverse organization was an indispensable part of a demographics-driven, customer-driven future" (Hesselbein, 2011, p. 72).

Next, we must listen. Seeing and listening, as Hesselbein so eloquently states, go hand in hand. After we see what is happening in our organizations or the world, we must ask questions and listen to others to be sure we *understand* what is happening. For example, Bill Pollard, former President and CEO of ServiceMaster talks about how seeing and listening enabled the growth of the company. In the 1980s, ServiceMaster was focused on health care institutions. However, school districts were becoming interested in the kinds of services provided by the company (plant operations and cleaning services). When the executive team was approached by managers within ServiceMaster with the idea of meeting the needs of schools, Pollard says:

> We were too busy with our own planning, listening to ourselves and not the customers. In fact, these managers were directed by me and others to get back to the work that was before them – to "stick to their knitting," and to continue to develop the health care market that we had before us and to let us at corporate get on with the strategic planning process . . . we thought we had the answers.
>
> *(1996, pp. 88–89)*

How did Pollard embrace a vision bigger than the one provided by the strategic planning process at ServiceMaster? He listened to the serious demands of lower level managers. One of the managers, Rich Williams, asked for permission to develop this line of business and put his entire annual salary on the table if he was not successful. While Pollard said it was a proposal they could not turn down, we beg to differ. Some managers would have certainly turned down this proposal and dinged Williams for not getting back to his "knitting." However, Williams' bold move caught the attention of the leadership at ServiceMaster because they listened. According to Pollard, schools became a major source of revenue for the company in a time when the health care business was stagnating.

Finally, to attain transcendence we must make connections to the world in ways that we have not done before. For example, in 2012, Paul Polman, CEO of Unilever, announced his vision for the organization's future. It is an aggressive and long-term plan to reduce the company's environmental impact by 50%. While his vision includes the profitability of Unilever, it importantly connects with the needs of people in the world and global challenges that threaten the long-term health of the planet. Polman states that the clear outcomes of the Unilever strategic plan will "help more than a billion people to improve their health and well-being; halve the environmental footprint of our products; [and] allow us to source 100% of our agricultural raw materials sustainably" (Unilever, n.d.). No one can deny this is a big vision. Yet, in a recent interview (Bird, 2010), Polman credits the role consumer activists play in helping businesses to see their responsibility to face challenging social problems rather than simply focus on shareholder returns. For him, listening to consumers helps to create the transcendent vision.

Be Ambitious for the Vision

Yet another misconception we noted while conducting our research about humility is that humble leaders do not think too highly of themselves and are thus not ambitious. That is, they do not reach for things outside of their grasp. Indeed, humility and ambition are often considered opposites. Certainly, one meaning of ambition is the "ardent desire for rank, fame or power," yet a second definition is a "desire to achieve a particular end" (Ambition, n.d.). Our study of humble leaders suggests that they are ambitious in the achieving of ends that are collectively beneficial. Jim Collins, author and leadership scholar, says of Frances Hesselbein, "she came in ... ambitious for the cause of the Girl Scouts" (Hesselbein, 2011, p. 207). To us, being an ambitious, humble leader means you believe in and move others toward a powerful *collective* vision. Hesselbein says:

> together we fashioned a vision. And we all caught fire with a powerful, distilled mission ... It had to do with helping each girl reach her own highest potential. We knew why we do what we do. And that was step one. We mobilized around vision and mission, had a couple of powerful goals that they helped develop. It was theirs.
>
> *(2011, p. 209)*

Hesselbein's quote suggests that being an ambitious, humble person results from being part of a community of people who embrace a powerful mission. Keith Grint of Warwick Business School states "leadership is the property and consequence of a community, rather than the property and consequence of an individual leader" (2005, p. 4). Humble leaders recognize the truth of this statement and work with people to refine and reframe vision so that followers are motivated to achieve the vision.

There is perhaps no better example of a great business leader who built a community committed to a vision than Mary Kay Ash. While Mary Kay had been successful as a training director in a large corporation, she felt that her career opportunities were limited because she was a woman. Mary Kay Cosmetics was born from a vision of creating "unlimited opportunity" for women (Ash, 1984, p. xvii). One of her tenets was to use the Golden Rule in creating company policy. According to Ash "Every people management decision made [at Mary Kay Cosmetics] is based on the Golden Rule" (Ash, 1984, p. 1). When Mary Kay was in sales, she thought territories were unfair because commissions were lost when people moved. For example, let's say you recruited and developed salespeople in Seattle but later moved to Tampa. In traditional sales organizations, a new manager would benefit from the recruits you developed in Seattle and you would have to recruit new folks in Tampa. At Mary Kay, however, you will receive commissions on your recruits no matter where you live. Additionally, they instituted an adoptee program where leaders develop recruits who were brought in by others (who have moved out of the region) although they will not receive commission for those recruits. When asked why this works, why people will develop someone for whom they will receive no commission, Mary Kay said:

> At Mary Kay Cosmetics . . . many sales directors who have as many as one hundred adoptees don't think that way [what's in it for me?]. Instead they think, "I'm helping them, but someone else is helping my recruits in another city" . . . when we began our adoptee program, it was generally felt that it wouldn't work. But I knew it would. I knew it would because it was based on the Golden Rule . . . it's a philosophy based on giving, and it is applied in every aspect of our business.
>
> *(Ash, 1984, p. 3)*

Mary Kay has created a community of people who are committed to a vision that is beyond what they will benefit from alone. They understand that they must think as a community and about the welfare of others.

Sacrifice Self

Finally, leading with humility on a daily basis requires self-sacrifice. What is sacrificial leadership? Researchers David De Cremer and his colleagues (2009) say that sacrificial leadership is evidenced when collective interests are privileged over personal interests. For example, sacrificial leaders would spend more time helping the team to achieve its objectives than pursuing their own career mobility, or sacrificial leaders may invest their personal financial resources in ensuring a team or business has the money needed to attain goals. Leaders may also give up perquisites associated with their position to share in the experiences of their followers.

In their work on sacrificial leadership, Yeon Choi and Renate Mai-Dalton (1998) relate the stories of a colonel in the Korean War who ate with the enlisted and washed his own tray. He could have eaten in the officers' mess hall and had a private clean up after him but he chose to put himself on the same level as his troops, to share their experiences. Similarly, Herb Kelleher designed the compensation system at Southwest Airlines so that corporate officers receive pay increases that are proportional to those received by other employees (Pandya & Shell, 2005). Moreover, when conditions demand it, officers take pay cuts. The question for a humble leader is not "Do I have the right to take advantage of a perk?" but "Should I exercise my rights to this perk at this time?"

Three Questions Humble Leaders should ask themselves Daily

Based on the research on sacrificial leadership (Choi & Mai-Dalton, 1998), we suggest three questions humble leaders can ask themselves each day:

1. *Am I taking the same kinds of risks I am asking others within the organization to take including risks associated with taking responsibility for failure, misfortunes, accidents, and mistakes?* Leaders who exercise humility *lead* the organization by taking appropriate responsibility for problems within the organization. When leaders blame subordinates for the organizational problems or ask followers to take risks to salary or personal lives while taking few (or none) themselves, then followers are likely to see leaders as believing their own livelihood and/or careers are worth protecting while those of followers are not.
2. *Is the distribution of awards appropriate?* Beyond the salaries that are paid, we would like for you to think about how appropriate the distribution of vacations, bonuses, and other perks are. For example, if you are paid much more than your subordinates, then you might consider whether the distribution of bonuses is appropriate. Warren Buffet has advanced this argument in talking about taxation. While he may pay more taxes than his secretary in real dollars, his rate of taxation is much smaller because his interest income is so large. Similarly, bonuses may mean much more to your subordinates because their salaries are so much smaller comparatively. Are you willing to forego certain benefits when others are experiencing hardship? Are you thinking about the differences in pay between you and your subordinates?
3. *Am I able to give up privileges, power, and resources which I have earned but should not exercise at this point in time in order to better lead the team?* At ServiceMaster,

all managers are required to train by doing "hands-on" work including janitorial services. Bill Pollard (1996) vividly recounts how his first six weeks as a senior executive included cleaning in hospitals and learning how to clean carpets and furniture. He was initially taken aback by the requirement but the chairman of the board and CEO explained that the experience of working in the field was essential to understanding the work lives of front line employees, to knowing the people and businesses he would manage. Pollard shares how he sometimes felt he lost his identity during the time he performed janitorial duties and how people talked about him while he was present as if he were invisible. Do executives within ServiceMaster have the power to end the field work socialization practice and to simply state that they contribute in different ways and therefore do not need to engage in *actual* cleaning? They absolutely could. However, humble leadership is sacrificial. It relinquishes its rights in order to lead better.

Reconciling Humility and Confidence: Humble Leaders *Are* Confident

At this juncture, you may be concerned about a seeming inconsistency between being humble and yet behaving confidently, being "leaderly." We know that it is commonly believed that leaders must always appear confident, so confessing to their strengths and weaknesses may seem to be the opposite of demonstrating a strong, self-possessed, leader persona. Yet, as we examined humble leaders we came to an important conclusion. Humble leaders *are* confident. According to the *American Heritage College Dictionary,* confidence is "trust or faith in a person or *thing*" (Pickett, 2001; emphasis ours). Indeed, we found that humble leaders base their confidence on the importance of the vision and their ability to lead the collective in attaining the vision. They know that they are committed to something significant and that they are "the person of the hour" who is responsible for and capable of bringing out the best in others interested in seeing the vision become a reality. Pollard may have said it best:

> Will the leader please stand up? Not the president, but the role model ... not the person who promotes himself, but the promoter of others ... People working together to perform a common objective need and want effective leadership—leadership they can trust—leadership that will nurture the soul.
>
> *(1996, p. 127)*

Leaders exercising humility are not people who say "I know I can do it—all of it—by myself if I must." Instead, leaders understand that they are promoting a vision that others want to see accomplished and that they need others to be involved. The vision is important enough to enlist others and keep them involved in seeing it to fruition. Therefore, the confidence of people who lead with humility comes from a place of understanding it isn't just about them. Their confidence has to be in a vision that brings people together to accomplish a common objective and to nurture the soul. So, what do you believe in? How far will you go to develop the people who are on the path with you?

Here are three ways to balance humility with confidence so that you have a clearer picture of how humble leaders practice confident humility.

Don't Run from Your Weaknesses

We became interested in Umpqua Bank, a community bank based in Portland, Oregon, because employees remarked on the quality of their leaders including behaviors we characterize as humble. Ray Davis, CEO, is particularly intriguing. While he and Umpqua have been very successful, Davis challenges leaders to be confident enough to acknowledge weakness—they are already exposed. He says:

> Most of the people you work with closely already see your weaknesses— probably more clearly than you do. And keeping people at a distance will only make you look weak and lacking in confidence. Sure, you take some risks exposing yourself, but there is really no alternative. Nobody is going to be led by a robot.
>
> *(Davis & Shrader, 2007, p. 100)*

We couldn't agree more. Glossing over weaknesses only makes leaders appear less trustworthy and perhaps less competent. After all, can you really lead others when you are blind to the areas that are a challenge for you? Humility allows you to be confident enough to admit weakness and smart enough to create structures (partners, etc.) to prevent that weakness from being a hindrance to achieving the mission.

Confidently Evaluate People against High Performance Standards

We believe that one of the concerns people have regarding leading with humility is that the leader is too weak to demand exemplary performance. The reasoning may go along these lines: Having admitted to my own weaknesses, how can I hold anyone else accountable? Hopefully, we have dispelled the myth about humility being synonymous with weakness throughout this book. Now, let's tackle the idea that a humble leader won't or can't hold people accountable.

"Leadership has to have power in order to empower," says William Pollard of ServiceMaster (Pollard, 1996, p. 101). We very much support this idea because we believe two things.

First, leadership only works when the led permit the leader to mobilize them toward a desired outcome (Heifetz, 1994). Leaders that are affirmed by the led have demonstrated that they are credible, competent, and trustworthy to lead. Second, leaders have established a collective vision that people believe is worth moving toward. If these two things are true, then accountability becomes essential but also possible because leader behaviors and the mission/vision become the standard against which people are evaluated.

Communicate Confidently and Humbly

As we examined humble leaders, we were particularly interested in how they communicated humbly *and* confidently. We think Mary Kay Ash says it well when she suggests the need for leaders to be tender and tough, to express empathy while remembering that their role is to lead people toward the objective. The humility in communication comes in sharing interdependence and weakness, being inclusive, and role-modeling transcendence. However, confident communication involves assuring followers that the organization is on the right path, must stay the course, and that you, as the leader, are committed to getting there. Humble leaders know how to communicate with followers such that the follower is committed—not because of manipulation—but because the vision is compellingly and confidently communicated. Moreover, the leader has exhibited such empathy, self-awareness, and inclusiveness that individuals are motivated to direct their energies toward the vision.

A Final Note: The Importance of Follower Attributions

To this point, we have given you five ways to behave humbly on a daily basis: seek to understand your strengths and weaknesses, share these with followers, embrace a vision larger than yourself, be ambitious for that vision, and appropriately sacrifice your own interests. We have also demonstrated that confidence and humility can co-exist. Yet, as you are behaving in these ways, you need to be able to know the extent to which your new behaviors are effective. Is your humility accomplishing results? Some may counter that they are being humble because it is simply the right thing to do. Of course it is. But, leading with humility is still about *leading*. It is still about motivating people toward a desired outcome—one that is collective, crafted in cooperation with followers through listening and seeing—but, at the end of the day, you are ambitious for a vision. You want to see something come into existence, changed, or eradicated.

Readers may be concerned that thinking about the "efficacy" of humility is the kind of "humility" that was displayed by Uriah Heep. Uriah Heep, in Charles Dickens' *David Copperfield*, extols his own humility yet all the while he is deviously undermining the interests of others, lying to them, and quietly advancing his own cause. He claims to be humble but his false humility is a cloak for a sinister heart. Eventually, people within the novel become aware of his duplicity and instigate his downfall. Clearly, we are not advocating that you use humility to advance your own cause (like Heep) and hasten your own doom. Instead we are suggesting that you behave humbly in order to advance a cause that you *and* your followers have envisioned or a vision that you have created and your followers have embraced. For example, Ruth Mompati, who served as Nelson Mandela's secretary before his imprisonment, says:

> What comes to my mind usually when I think of Nelson is that he is a unique person. He is fearless and yet he's got humility. I am sometimes surprised that a man who could have had so much gave it away because he wanted freedom for himself and his people . . .
>
> He has lived a good life in that he's done his utmost in relation to his aspirations to bring change to South Africa.
>
> *(Maharaj & Kathrada, 2006, p. 57)*

Mompati recognized self-sacrifice, a humble behavior in Mandela. She recognized this behavior was self-interested but also others-interested. Of course he wanted freedom for people of color in South Africa, but he also wanted freedom himself. Finally, she saw that he embraced a vision—larger than himself— of bringing change to South Africa.

Why are follower attributions important? Our research suggests that when followers *believe* a leader is acting with authentic humility, then commitment, self-efficacy, trust in the leader, motivation, and follower willingness to sacrifice in pursuit of the vision are all positively impacted. As we discuss in Chapter 8, leader humility may positively impact follower self-efficacy or one's confidence in their ability to perform a task (Bandura, 1986; Gist, 1989). Leaders need to be interested in self-efficacy because when people feel confident in their ability, they are more willing to accept difficult goals, to put effort into goal attainment, and to persist in pursuit of goals despite obstacles (Bandura, 1997). Put simply, they significantly outperform others who are without self-efficacy. As we have talked with and studied leaders and followers, we see that a leader's ability to act with humility— especially to admit weakness—positively influences followers' self-efficacy. Why? Because when leaders honestly admit to weakness in an area where followers are strong and encourage followers to bring their strengths to bear in attaining the vision, they are engaging in a form of verbal persuasion and affirmative coaching.

In sum, followers need to see and attribute humility to leaders. They may not use the word "humility" but they see that their leaders aren't afraid to admit weakness, to be teachable, to affirm strengths in others, and to admit their dependence on the talents of followers. Followers need to see the leader as less concerned with their own interests and passionate for the vision. When followers see "humility" in the leader, they follow and great things happen.

Conclusion

We started this chapter by stating that while many people are highly intrigued by the idea of humble leadership, it's very difficult to wrap one's head around how to actually be a humble leader. The purpose of this chapter is to clear up some common misconceptions about how leaders exercising humility may behave. We suggested that five behaviors are extremely important: seeking to know and share your understanding of your strengths and weaknesses, embracing a vision larger than yourself, being ambitious for that vision, and appropriately sacrificing your own interests. We also demonstrated that humility and confidence can and do co-exist in outstanding business and social enterprise leaders. Our goal is not to make you an inauthentic leader, but to demonstrate to you that (just like your muscle tone) humility can be developed by exercising a little each day. Of course, it's not easy. But once acquired, humility will allow you to lead more effectively, enable your followers to recognize your humility, and accomplish meaningful and long-lasting results in your organization.

CASE STUDY: WALK THE TALK BUT DON'T FORGET TO TALK THE WALK

Should Leaders Attempting to Exercise Humility Communicate Their Attempts at Being Humble to Followers?

In the latter part of this chapter, we exposed you to a new idea. Leaders who exhibit humility aren't afraid to let their followers (and others) know that they are attempting to exercise humility. In essence, they manage their displays of humility. We understand that this might be a troubling thought. You may think of the attempt to manage perceptions as manipulative and not likely to be seen in a humble leader. We ask you to suspend disbelief. Instead, consider for a moment that you have a big vision—one that, in many ways could change the world. However, it is not a popular vision. Indeed, it is one that many people claim to be counter to nature and detrimental to the nation. Could impression management be important in such a situation? To examine this question further, we present Martin Luther King, Jr., a leader who fits our definition of humility.

Our case on King provides you with a few passages from his speeches (or other writings), our interpretations of those passages, and a few questions for you to ponder. Remember, you don't have to decide today if King was humble or if humility impressions can be managed. Rather, we invite you to think.

Thoughts on Exercising and Managing Humility

As we read through King's papers, we were struck by his understanding of the need to have a message that was spread far and wide. He shared the following ideas regarding propaganda.

> For the average person, the word propaganda has evil and vicious overtones. Propaganda is considered something used by the demagogue to spread evil ideologies . . . But propaganda does not have to be evil. There is a noble sense in which propaganda can be used . . . In the 1 chapter of the book of Acts, Jesus is reported to have said to his disciples, "ye shall be witnesses unto me in Jerusalem, and in all Judea, and in Samaria, and unto the uttermost part of the earth" . . . Jesus is calling upon his disciples to be true propagandizers. He is saying in effect, propagandize my word, spread it, disseminate it, push it into every nock and crok of the universe, carry it to every tribe and every race, every nation and every village; propagandize my word to the uttermost part of the earth.
>
> *(King & Carson, 2007, p. 184)*

Someone might suggest a humble person would not extol propaganda because they do not wish to call attention to themselves. We agree that leaders exercising humility do not seek to call attention to themselves. However, leaders who exercise humility absolutely want their message to be spread. They want their disciples to be sure that the word is out because the vision is that important. The leader is not central but the message is and because of that truth, the leader must spread the message.

It is also clear that King emphasized the life of humility—a focus on the mission rather than self-interest. For example, in a sermon he shares:

> many people feel inferior because they have their egos on their hands. The ego stands out as a sore thumb, oversensitive and easily hurt. The thing that individuals must do somehow is to push the ego in the background by becoming absorbed in great causes and in great ideals and in great principles. I think this is what Jesus meant when he said, "He who seeks to find his life shall lose it, and he who loses his life for my sake shall find it." In other words, he who seeks to find his ego will

lose his ego, but he who loses his ego in some great cause greater than his ego shall find his ego. This is the thing that challenges us.

(King & Carson, 2007, p. 314)

Finally, as we read through the letters and sermons of King, we believe his writings changed over time becoming more personal, more reflective. Moreover, as early as 1960, he began to discuss the possibility that he may not live long but he does not lose his desire to keep in mind the transcendent nature of the movement. It was bigger than him. To this end, he seemed more open to sharing his weaknesses and his fears in his writings as the Civil Rights Movement developed and physical, legal, and mental dangers multiplied. Note this story:

> During the bus protest in Montgomery, Alabama, one of the most dedicated participants was an elderly Negro woman that we affectionately called Mother Pollard. Although poverty-stricken and uneducated, she was amazingly intelligent and possessed a deep understanding of the meaning of the movement . . . One Monday evening, after having gone through a tension-packed week which included being arrested and receiving numerous threatening calls, I went to the mass meeting depressed and fear-stricken. In my address I tried desperately to give an overt impression of strength and courage but deep down within the soil of my inner life was the nagging serpent of fear which left me poisoned with the fangs of depression. At the end of the meeting, Mother Pollard came to the front of the church and said, "Come here son . . . something is wrong with you. You didn't talk strong tonight." Seeking to keep my fears to myself, I retorted, "Oh, no, Mother Pollard, nothing is wrong. I am feeling as fine as ever." "Now you can't fool me," she said. "I knows something is wrong. Is it that we aint doing things to please you? or is it that the white folks is bother you?" Before I could answer she looked directly into my eyes and said, "I don told you we is with you all the way." And then with a countenance beaming with quiet certainty she concluded, "but even if we aint with you, God's gonna take care of you." Everything in me quivered with the pulsing tremor of raw energy when she uttered these consoling words.
>
> *(King & Carson, 2007, p. 544)*

In sharing this story, King pulls back the curtain on his own fears and weakness, his utter interdependence with the crowd, and his spiritual reliance on God. He shared himself with people in a way that motivated them to follow him.

For your consideration, we offer the following questions:

- What might the passages above mean to followers during the height of the Civil Rights Movement?
- What action might they encourage in followers?
- Now that you have read this case study, how does it apply to your own exercise of humility in leadership?

8

WHY HUMILITY MATTERS

Empowering Followers

> I start with the premise that the function of leadership is to produce more leaders not more followers.
>
> *Ralph Nader, American political activist*

Empowerment: An Example

When was the last time you had a customer service issue? It's not typically thought of as a fun experience. Have you ever had an exchange with an employee who wasn't able to resolve a problem—a return, for example? Many of us have escalated the situation by asking to speak with a manager. After all, we needed a resolution and the employee either didn't want to give us what we wanted, or, as is often the case, simply couldn't give us what we wanted because it was not in his purview to do so.

Companies and leaders that empower employees take a different approach. Zappos is a good example. The largest online shoe retailer, "Zappos is about delivering happiness to the world" (Hsieh, 2010, p. 230, as cited in Leslie & Aaker, 2010). They have created a lot of happiness for a lot of their customers by empowering their employees. New Zappos employees spend two weeks early on in their training taking calls from customers. Zappos employees don't receive a script; instead, they are encouraged to take as much time as needed to resolve any customer service issues. Moreover, Zappos employees have the option of engaging in a corporate training program that enables them to develop 20 skill sets. Employees are not required to take the training, but each time they do, they are rewarded with a small pay increase (Leslie & Aaker, 2010). The employees get to decide how the customer's problem will be resolved and the employees are able to partake in training courses at their own pace.

We believe that leaders who exercise humility are uniquely well positioned to help their followers experience the joys of true empowerment, as well as other positive outcomes such as increased engagement in their work, positive identification with and trust in their leader, and a sense of psychological freedom about themselves and their capabilities. As such, this chapter first discusses what empowerment is. We then cover strategies leaders can use for enhancing follower self-efficacy and achieving higher motivation from followers. To that end, this chapter will help leaders develop a solid and productive relationship with followers and enhance follower confidence and autonomy so they can make decisions on whether or not they want to work toward mission achievement. Finally, we conclude with a brief discussion of other positive outcomes beyond empowerment that leaders with humility may inspire in their followers.

Empowerment Defined

Empowerment is the process of increasing follower self-efficacy levels by recognizing and removing conditions that create powerlessness, including increasing autonomy (Conger & Kanungo, 1988; Pearce & Conger, 2003). Self-efficacy, the concept coined by world-renowned psychologist Albert Bandura, reflects a follower's confidence in his/her ability to carry out a task successfully (Bandura, 1997). While at first this might not sound all that exciting, the implications of higher self-efficacy are significant as we'll outline in the section below. Scholars have noted that the most important behaviors that leaders can demonstrate to enhance their empowerment of followers are trust and facilitation (Howard & Wellins, 1994 as cited in Bass & Bass, 2008). Other empowerment behaviors include supporting, coaching, inspiring, and team building (Howard & Wellins, 1994, as cited in Bass & Bass, 2008). Let's look more closely at the impact of empowerment on followers and consider *how* leaders empower others.

Why It's Important: Empowerment's Effect on Followers

For followers, being empowered means that they get to be in charge of and own certain decisions. Simply stated, followers who are empowered feel potent. They get to have a voice and are enabled to engage critical thinking skills when coming up with a path forward on an issue or a solution. The impact this has on followers is impressive. A study on empowerment found that employees reported feeling more positive about their work and experienced less work related stress (Howard & Wellins, 1994, as cited in Bass & Bass, 2008). Scholars Kirkman and Rosen (1999) similarly find that empowered teams feel more potent and autonomous, and experience their work as more meaningful and impactful.

Empowered followers are not only satisfied followers; they are confident followers (Conger & Kanungo, 1988). Enhancing follower confidence (i.e., self-efficacy) might not seem all that important at first glance. Yet research findings are robust and powerfully clear: assuming equal ability and equal resources, higher confidence in one's ability to perform a task translates into higher performance on that task in nearly all cases (see Bandura, 1997, for a review). This means that if you step onto a basketball court tomorrow to face an opponent with commensurate ability and you both have equal access to the proper equipment (loose fitting clothing, a decent pair of hi-tops, and a regulation size ball and net), simply having more confidence in yourself than your opponent has in him/herself secures your victory. This is because individuals with higher levels of confidence set higher goals for themselves, persist longer in the face of obstacles as they pursue those goals, view challenges as opportunities for learning and growth, and experience less anxiety and stress as compared to those with lower self-efficacy (see Bandura, 1997). This means you'll likely shoot more, take higher risks, feel less nervous, and persist longer than your competitor. And all that translates into more points on the scoreboard at the end of the game. Fortunately, the positive impacts of self-efficacy aren't limited to recreational sports; work on self-efficacy and its consequences is supported in many disciplines, including psychology, education, health, and management, to name just a few (Bandura, 1997).

Going Further: Leading with Humility to Develop Follower Self-Efficacy

Bandura's (1997) classic research discusses four primary ways self-efficacy can be taught. We present these below for leaders who wish to empower followers through enhancing the followers' self-efficacy. We also offer specific ways in which leading with humility uniquely contributes to self-efficacy building techniques.

Verbal persuasion (Bandura, 1997)—A simple tactic to elevate follower self-efficacy is for the leader to express *their* authentic confidence in the follower. One way to do this is by articulating high expectations, such as setting challenging, specific, yet achievable goals. Presenting followers with such goals is a statement that, in itself, signals the leader's belief in their follower's capability. When genuine, those signals can have a big impact. Moreover, following up with timely and positive feedback will enhance follower confidence even further (Bandura, 1997). Because key elements of effective verbal persuasion include credible and genuine statements of leaders' belief in their followers' capabilities, we believe that the relational orientation held by leaders with humility is likely to result in high-quality, honest interchanges between leader and follower and sets the stage for effective verbal persuasion. Additionally, we believe that humble leaders are more likely to view their role in relationships with followers as a "coach" who is concerned about the welfare of others and recognizes the positive impact their verbal persuasion can have on follower well-being. A humble leader's vote of confidence in his/her follower might mean "just that much more" than statements from leaders who are not as invested in their relationships with followers.

Enactive mastery (Bandura, 1997)—Enactive mastery means that as followers master tasks and experience successes, their efficacy levels will also rise. Leaders who utilize this technique break down larger tasks into smaller, more manageable "chunks" and provide followers with helpful ideas and task-appropriate strategies that guide followers toward early success. Because seeing the larger picture is a critical prerequisite for setting up opportunities for enactive mastery to occur, the perspective taking and holding of humble leaders should provide them with the resources, ideas, and inclination needed for this technique.

Vicarious experience (Bandura, 1997)—Imagine this scenario: Your best friend challenges you to bench-press 50lbs. You are a slender female who doesn't regularly lift weights at the gym. At this point, your self-efficacy with respect to this task is likely rather low. The next morning, however, while on your way to the treadmill, you take a look over at the weight section and you see another female, approximately your same build and age. She is easily bench-pressing 50lbs! After seeing this, it is highly probable that your efficacy levels were elevated just by virtue of observing a credible, "like-other" succeeding at the task at hand. When leaders are interested in elevating self-efficacy through this "vicarious experience of success" technique, they strategically set up arrangements and partnerships that provide followers with ample opportunities to work directly with successful "like-others," learn from them, and experience a taste of their success vicariously. Alternatively, through mirroring back to a follower *the follower's own* successes and strengths (and only strengths), leaders can also achieve similar self-efficacy building effects. Interestingly, it is unclear if leading with humility allows leaders any advantages in exercising this technique for their followers given its focus solely on strengths.

Psychological states/Emotional arousal (Bandura, 1997)—This fourth and final technique rests on the relationship between one's perceptions of their internal state and their confidence levels. Followers are more likely to expect success when not burdened with stress, tension, or other agitating feelings. Thus, when leaders arouse positive states such as excitement in followers, and minimize adverse states such as anxiety, they help to build higher motivation and performance in their followers. Leaders can also help followers to correct misinterpretations of stress or other adverse internal states so that they are not as debilitating; for instance, a leader who helps followers to focus on issues that are within the followers' control (rather than external forces that are not) may effectively help followers cope with stress and enhance confidence levels. We suspect that leaders who lead with humility are likely to arouse positive internal states in their followers and to do so frequently because leading with humility often means listening to followers, viewing followers as part of an interdependent relationship, and explaining to them why their ideas are or are not included within the leader's vision.

To raise a follower's sense of self-efficacy any of the above four techniques will work. We recommend that you pick one or two that either fit most closely to your personal style and/or are most likely to be accepted within your current organizational culture and give them a try. In doing so, remember that changes often take some time and persistence to "stick"; you may need to try the same technique a few times over before you can assess in what ways it is working (for you and for your different followers). And, finally, if you are a leader who is cultivating his/her humility, be sure to draw upon the strengths that your humility affords to be even more genuine and impactful in your efforts toward empowering followers.

Bettering Followers: Outcomes beyond Empowerment

Below, we draw upon extant research and discuss several anticipated outcomes of leading with humility. After reading the list and descriptions, please take a moment to compare and contrast these with the kinds of outcomes that you would like to see as a leader, or a follower. A few questions might arise for you while you reflect. Can humble leaders develop and extend their followers' capabilities beyond other leaders? Does leading with humility always lead to anticipated outcomes for followers that are reflective of empowered followership? When might it not? Is this good for the follower, the leader, the organization?

Identification (Nielsen, et al., 2010)—We expect that followers will positively identify with a humble leader and his/her vision. Followers will see their leaders as possessing and demonstrating self-awareness, an awareness of their relationship with others, and achieving a larger perspective.

Trust (Nielsen, et al., 2010)—Due to their humility, we suspect that followers of leaders with humility will trust their leader. These followers believe in the leader and they believe that the leader is going to do what they say they are going to do. Trust is important to the follower–leader relationship because both are going to be investing time and energy in working together.

Self-efficacy (Nielsen, et al., 2010)—As suggested by the above, we expect that followers of leaders with humility tend to have high levels of self-efficacy.

Follower engagement (Owens & Hekman, 2012)—Followers of humble leaders have been found to be more engaged with their jobs than those being led by non-humble leaders (Owens & Hekman, 2012). These followers find that their interactions with a leader with humility encourage them to extend more effort and persist longer in performing tasks. Owens and Hekman suggest these followers are more intrinsically motivated than followers of non-humble leaders.

Willingness to sacrifice (Nielsen, et al., 2010)—Followers of leaders with humility are expected to demonstrate temporary acts of self-sacrifice, such as foregoing personal benefits (e.g., higher paying jobs) because they see their leader doing the same. In doing so, these followers realize that they are working toward goals that are greater than themselves and are thus less focused on self-gratification.

Psychological freedom (Owens & Hekman, 2012)—Leaders provide their followers with a safe space to be vulnerable. Followers are thus able to express themselves, not only because the leaders says it's okay to be transparent, but also because leaders with humility demonstrate this transparency through their own admission of limitations and strengths. This psychological freedom helps followers feel more comfortable with who they are and what capabilities they possess.

Concluding Thoughts

Empowered followers are a hallmark of leaders with humility. This chapter looked at the benefits of empowerment for followers. We then outlined the ways in which leaders with humility can behave to develop empowerment in followers and to develop follower self-efficacy. We concluded by considering several other proposed outcomes of leading with humility. For established and aspiring leaders who are interested in cultivating their humility and helping followers grow, the next chapter provides exercises to develop one's own humility as a leader.

CASE STUDY: EMPOWERING FOLLOWERS

How Do Humble Leaders Influence Follower Self-Efficacy?

The founder of Roots of Empathy, Mary Gordon, is a leader in the movement to build empathy in children and, by extension, in society. Her journey began as a kindergarten teacher where she became convinced that early childhood experiences set children on paths toward success or failure. However, Gordon is not simply interested in the academic success of children. She is interested in their success as human beings. She describes a transcendent vision of the value of public education:

> Public education is the basis of a healthy democracy. Working in schools, I saw how crucial it is that we teach children to ask questions and help them find a voice. Voice is bound up in their confidence and feelings of self-worth and is key to their future as citizens who will take their place in a democratic society . . . the goal of education is broader than creating job-ready youth—it involves nurturing individuals who can be publicly useful and personally fulfilled. Education has a responsibility to develop citizens.
>
> *(Gordon, 2009, p. xix)*

Many public school educators, politicians, and taxpaying citizens in countries offering public education would agree. However, few seem to agree on the means to accomplishing a public education that attends to the intellectual and moral development of children. What makes Gordon different and worth our consideration here? The answer is her "411" approach. She has determined that education starts by working with parents in a way that evokes our definition of humility. She shares:

> Parents are naturally loath to attend programs that tell them "how to be a good parent." The parenting program we initiated came from a different premise, from a position of respect for parents and a belief that they want to do their best for their children. The parents we began with were seen as having strengths and experiences they could share with one another. The worker in the parenting center was a facilitator and a catalyst. At that time, most other programs started with the assumption that they were there to fix a deficit. Their message was that parents were failing, and their program had an expert who would provide all the answers to their problems. I believe strongly in taking a "411" rather than "emergency rescue" or "911" approach. A "911" approach is about rescuing, reclaiming, recovering—after the damage is done—and it inevitably falls far short of the mark . . . a "411" approach: a resource, not a rescue mission.
>
> *(Gordon, 2009, p. 233)*

Gordon's "411" approach begins by removing conditions that contribute to powerlessness—namely a lack of resources but, perhaps, more importantly a lack of empathy *for parents—not just children*. Gordon doesn't join with the throngs of people criticizing parents. Instead, she empathizes with the struggles of parents who have little resources or help in their quest to parent effectively. Her goal is to create a "supportive, nonjudgmental community" (Gordon, 2009, p. 233) where parents can belong and experience help.

But, does it work? Are families empowered? Are children able to develop the skills needed for citizenship? According to research by Kimberly Schonert-Reichl and Fiona Scott, the answer is "yes." The pair, along with colleagues Clyde Hertzman, Veronica Smith, and Anat Zaidman-Zait, conducted research to determine the efficacy of Gordon's program on outcomes. They found that children engaged in the program were "more advanced in the social and emotional understanding" compared with children not experiencing the program. Moreover, children engaged in roots of empathy (ROE) showed decreases in aggression and increases in caring, kindness, and peer acceptance. ROE children had greater ability to take perspective and reported higher levels of classroom supportiveness (Gordon, 2009).

For your consideration, we offer the following questions:

- Does Mary Gordon's leadership suggest the exercise of leadership humility to you? Why or why not?
- In what ways do you think parents and children are empowered as a result of ROE's leadership?

9

CULTIVATING HUMBLE LEADERSHIP

Do you wish to be great? Then begin by being. Do you desire to construct a vast and lofty fabric? Think first about the foundations of humility. The higher your structure is to be, the deeper must be its foundation.

Saint Augustine

When we began to conceive of this chapter, we drew a mental picture of cultivation and thought about what it would mean to *cultivate* humility. Let us take you where we began.

Imagine yourself standing at the end of a barren field in the waning days of winter. The ground is hard and packed tight. Out of the corner of your eye, you see a huge piece of farm equipment outfitted with large spikes that dig into the ground turning and breaking up the soil. You stop the driver of the farm equipment and ask the purpose of this exercise. "What are you doing?" The driver answers, "Unless I break the ground up, the seeds we wish to plant will not take root. The ground is so hard that the seedlings would not be able to pierce it and grow into the crops we need. We could never have a harvest without first breaking up the ground."

The generic term for this kind equipment is "cultivator." You might have a rototiller or a shovel at home that you use in your backyard garden. Regardless of what implement comes to mind, we hope you now have a clear picture of what it means to cultivate. It is to prepare ground, to break up soil so that something may grow. This chapter is about breaking up the ground in our minds and hearts that prevents us from exercising humility in leadership. We present the exercises within this chapter as rototillers, shovels, cultivators that dig around (might hurt a little bit) and prepare you to be a more humble leader.

You may ask: "Can one cultivate humility? Isn't the very attempt to cultivate humility the beginning of its demise?" These are both outstanding questions.

Certainly, there are some who see it this way (Krishnamurthi, 2009). In contrast, positive psychology researchers suggest there are interventions that may facilitate the development of humility (Peterson & Seligman, 2004). Our perspective, based on this research and our own, is that the desire and act of becoming more virtuous is a good thing. We compare it to the drive toward mastery as described by Daniel Pink. Pink (2011) compares attempts to attain mastery to an asymptote (which is a curve that very nearly approaches a straight line but never quite makes it). Mastery is something that you never fully attain though you can get close. We'd like to suggest that cultivating humility is similar to mastery in this respect—it is something one strives for but cannot achieve. Therefore, we cede some agreement with those who say attempting to become humble keeps one from becoming humble. However, we also argue that attempting to develop humility takes you closer to becoming and displaying humility than you would have been otherwise. We simply cannot agree that *not* seeking to be humble will enable humility.

Even more importantly, we'd like to assert that it may be possible to rethink humility (as we have done throughout this book) and see it not simply as a virtuous state (which one may never fully achieve) but as a set of behaviors that one

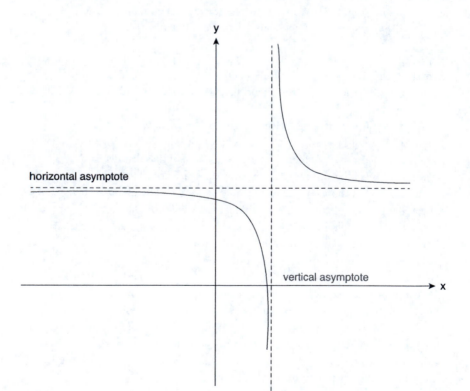

FIGURE 9.1 Asymptote

can exercise out of a desire to develop others, achieve a transcendent vision, and to be the best leader one can be. Our focus in this chapter is on cultivating humility by using exercises that cause one to behave with humility.

The exercises discussed in this chapter are about developing habits of the heart, mind, and hands that demonstrate humility. Our exercises fall into three broad categories: building a relational identity orientation, engaging in reflective practice (to better understand strengths and weaknesses), and employing behavioral practices (relational and perspective taking leader activities). We have provided exercises in each category that we believe will help in the cultivation of humility.

Establishing a Relational Identity Orientation

By this point, you will have realized that leading with humility is really about being a relational leader. Our prescriptions are centered on the relationship between you and those who would follow you. For example, you have to recognize your interdependence with others. You need to share your strengths and weaknesses. You need to embrace a vision that is bigger than yourself, one that you share with your followers. Therefore, leading with humility requires the development of a relational identity orientation. Scholars Shelley Brickson and Marilynn Brewer (2001) define a relational identity orientation as present when the source of self-definition is characterized by concern for the welfare of others and when role standards are often used for comparison. Brickson and Brewer suggest that people evaluate themselves in terms of their skill in performing interpersonal roles. Moreover, they state that a relational orientation suggests cooperative interdependence where the well-being of each party is enhanced by the other. Leaders who exercise humility want to foster relationships where people are concerned about each other's welfare. Exercises 1 and 2 provide interventions to build your ability to construct a relational orientation.

Exercise 1—Embracing a Vision Larger than Oneself

The steps that follow in this first exercise are useful for situations when you are crafting your own vision or in situations when an edict has been handed down to you. For the latter, imagine you didn't get to craft a vision at all. The vision is what it is. People often lament about this reality. In classes, we sometimes hear people ask: "What do you do when the vision is not *your* vision? I don't agree with the vision dreamed up by upper management but I have to carry it out." We believe there are at least two courses of action, both of which can help people embrace a vision that is larger than themselves. First, we suggest that people share their concerns with organizational leaders. Some may counter: "Well that's useless. They're headed in a particular direction and that's it." Okay (although we do note that concerns voiced in some circumstances may be listened to and may help one to feel better). Next, we recommend that people find something they *can* be passionate about within the vision so that they can lead their teams or functions in fulfilling the vision.

Here's a concrete example that we will use to demonstrate this exercise. Imagine that you work for an organization that envisions using methods such as TQM, 5S, Kaizen, or Six Sigma to improve organizational outcomes. Organizational leaders believe that using such a program will enable the organization to achieve higher quality. However, as you listen to the plans to implement the new program, you realize the application of TQM or Six Sigma does not really seem to fit the organization. The change does not seem appropriate. In fact, you are concerned the change will increase worker dissatisfaction as the logic for change is unclear and the resources required to implement the changes have not been provided. What would you do as a leader exercising humility who wanted to embrace a vision larger than self if one of these programs was planned but you saw important issues that would prevent effective implementation?

Step 1: Ask questions of yourself and others. We suggest:

* Why are we doing what we are doing?
* What facts, figures, or stories influenced our leadership to construct this vision?
* What is the desired end state? Why?

Step 2: If you truly want to embrace a vision larger than yourself, get out of your office to explore the answers to the above questions. If the answer to the question "Why are we doing this?" is "To better serve customers," then arrange to speak with customers. If the answer is "Costs are skyrocketing and Six Sigma, Kaizen, or 5S will help to lower costs," then explore the metrics that will enable you to understand and share the link between the program and costs. Perhaps the answer is in the form of a story about an organization that used one of the programs in a similar application and achieved unexpected and amazing results. Study the benchmark story to understand the similarities and differences between that organization and yours. You might even visit the company. We encourage you to connect within and outside of your organization to better understand the vision.

Step 3: Think about what makes you passionate within the scope of the vision and determine how you can bring your passion to bear on the current problem. Perhaps, after all of this work, you decide that you still don't agree with the vision. As a result, your goal might be to implement the system in a way that doesn't demotivate your group resulting in poor performance and counter-productive work behaviors. We'd say this (focusing on the needs of your group) is a vision that is bigger than your personal interests. Think about how you can bring this passion to bear on implementing change in your organization.

The steps above don't change much if you get to start from scratch with a vision of your own choosing. There is something in the world, your organization, or your team that needs changing. Start first with the current state of the world. Then ask yourself, "Why does it exist?" Follow up with getting out of your office (comfort zone) to understand what others are experiencing. Finally, end by discovering what has made you passionate about the issue and how you can bring your passion to bear on the problem.

Exercise 2—Visioning: Adopting a Humble Stance and Enlisting and Engaging Others in a Relational Vision

Exercise 2 is for leaders who are starting new projects, joining a new group as its leader, or needing to revitalize a team that has lost direction or momentum. Again, we'll use a practical example to illustrate. However, before we launch into the exercise itself, we want to state that this exercise is the result of much debate and deliberation. We grappled with how leaders can enlist people in vision setting that isn't impractical, ineffective, or unfair. We've each read books and research studies. Some of us have discussed visioning with students. Moreover, we live in organizations where visioning takes place continuously. So, we know what it's like to try to create vision and to be engaged in vision exercises. We've decided that there are four primary reasons this area is difficult:

1. Leaders have real outcomes that they wish to see achieved. While the vision isn't only about leaders, it is at least a little about leaders and what they want to see accomplished. So, how *do* leaders create a vision that includes what *they* want and incorporates the aspirations of others?
2. Visioning is ongoing and dynamic—although it may not appear so. Visioning doesn't just happen when a team gets chartered or at the beginning of an initiative. The environment is shaping our thinking and those thoughts are contributing to the vision.
3. Although the objective is to get everyone rowing in the same direction, the reality is that not everyone will embrace a vision at the very beginning. And you know what? We don't think that takes anything away from your leadership or your humility. There are a number of possible reasons for this. For example, people may not quite understand how the vision will impact them. Past organizational politics or history may cloud the ability to embrace new visions (the "I've been burned before" syndrome).
4. You may stumble in the process. You'll include a number of people but not everyone may have a chance to voice their concerns initially because of time constraints, legal requirements that things be done as confidentially as possible (at least in the beginning), or because the processes we suggest are unfamiliar to you. When you stumble, you may conclude this just doesn't

work. We ask that you keep trying. As clichéd as it may sound, practice does lead to improvement.

With all of these things in mind, we've crafted an exercise that builds on what we've learned (and debated) about crafting a relational vision. The exercise begins with considering a practical example that helps us to reframe visioning. In countries like the United States, many workers have been involved in writing vision and mission statements. Often, this can be a rewarding and enriching experience that allows employees to identify more strongly with their organization and its mission. However, we have found that some people feel disengaged from this process because the process seems disconnected from organizational goals and day-to-day work or because the exercise of crafting the vision itself seems unduly burdened with wordsmithing and seemingly meaningless arguments over semantics. Yet, Shelley Kirkpatrick's (2009) research has demonstrated the value of a communicated vision statement for good follower and organization outcomes. Her research would predict that vision statements are most effective when there is goal alignment, followers are confident in their ability to achieve the vision, the language used in the statement gets everyone on the same page, and followers see the vision as challenging and meaningful. Therefore, the challenge is to have a visioning process and write vision statements that leave people energized rather than demoralized.

To do this and create the kinds of visioning processes we've discussed above, we propose a new way to think about the creation of vision. In our conceptualization, visioning is a group decision process and the outcome, the vision, reflects the needs and desires of the people involved. As such, there are two possible approaches to decision making (Garvin & Roberto, 2001). The first approach is *advocacy* where the purpose of visioning is to get people to move in a particular direction and leaders to defend their positions and present them as the strongest or best direction. In contrast, one can take an *inquiry* based approach where people are engaged in "collaborative problem solving" that leads to shared ownership of the decision. Throughout this exercise, we frame visioning as an inquiry based decision making process. Three key steps are involved.

Step 1: Iterate between a blank slate and your vision.

During the process, listen. What concerns do people have about moving in the direction of the vision? What are their fears? What energizes them about the vision? What outcomes excite them?

It's hard to imagine where you should start, isn't it? We suggest that you iterate between a blank slate (let organizational members completely drive the vision) and your proposal for the vision. For example, if you are attempting to create a new strategic direction as a service provider, you may have a good idea of the environment because of market research. In this case, you may share this market information and your vision for the future direction of the organization. In contrast, as a community leader, you may not want to suggest a vision for reducing crime in your neighborhood. Instead, you may believe that the neighborhood must decide and, therefore, start with a blank slate. Thus, we think it is possible to start either with a blank slate or your vision— as long as all three key steps in the exercise are followed.

Should you start with your vision, you will still need to learn what the people you lead need to become passionate about the vision. You may notice we said "people" rather than organization or team. We are purposeful in suggesting you think about the individuals you are leading rather than just the organization or team as whole. Ask yourself: What do the people I lead need to understand and execute the vision? What is going to make people passionate about where we're going? It is important to recognize that different people will hear your vision differently and will react with different emotions and questions. They almost certainly won't feel passionate about the same aspects of the vision that you find intriguing. After all, you and they are looking at the future from two very different vantage points. You're the leader standing on the mountain top. Your followers are in the valley trying to understand the vista as you describe it but seeing the same landscape they've always seen. Don't be surprised if people need to be engaged and included to feel the passion about the vision that has lit your fire. This begins with listening.

Should you start with a blank state (or even with your vision), you should expect that there will be disagreements concerning the direction. Thus, let's take a moment to talk about constructive conflict using our example of the community leader. Neighbors may not agree on the sources of crime or the remedies. They may not all see the police as helpful or feel that neighborhood watches are effective. As long as people are engaged in debating ideas related to the tasks at hand, conflict can be extremely useful (Amason, 1996; DeDreu, 2006; Jehn, 1997). Welcome the conflict. Step 2 will help you with this further.

Step 2: Develop a process to include people in debating and discussing the vision. Garvin and Roberto (2001) suggest that you structure decision making groups into two bodies. As a leader exercising humility, we think enabling a real debate that allows for questioning different views is essential. For example, let's say you do have a strategic vision for the future of the organization. One subgroup of your followers could present your view by sharing the assumptions underpinning the vision. Another subgroup could present another proposed vision for the future. During the debate, groups question the underlying assumptions and work together to develop a common set of recommendations. The key to this debate is ensuring that everyone's input is considered, not necessarily agreed upon.

We think this process has the potential for great efficacy for leaders exercising humility. In the end, you do not think of influence as a one way street. Humble leadership is relational. You listened to your followers in Step 1. You listened because you wanted to understand and address their concerns—to the best of your ability. As you influence, be sure to share that you heard their concerns and that you have managed their concerns as best you could and as appropriate. Even if you do not engage in a formal process of two subgroups, build in time for people to question assumptions and seek to provide real answers or change the assumptions when a good answer is not forthcoming.

Step 3: Create a role that defines followers within the organization. Share the standards for successfully performing the role (followers may help create this). Develop metrics for determining the extent to which people are successfully fulfilling their roles/commitments to one another.

Here in Step 3, focus people on roles. A relational orientation and relational vision should encourage people to evaluate themselves according to a role standard. For example, Frances Hesselbein, former CEO of the Girl Scouts, kept people thinking about their relationships to the girls in Girl Scouting. You want people to define themselves in terms of their relationships to others and then to determine whether or not they are fulfilling that role appropriately. Therefore, you might encourage people to think of themselves as teammates, colleagues, or service providers. Each of which is a relationally oriented identity. Then, you want them to develop a metric, based on norms for performing those roles, for evaluating their performance. "Am I a good teammate or colleague based on our definition of that role?"

Engaging in Reflective Practice

The authors of this book are faculty or alumni of Seattle University, a Jesuit institution. For Jesuits, the practice of reflection is central to the idea of becoming just and humane persons. Thus, influenced by our Jesuit roots and positive psychology research, we also emphasize the essential role of reflection in cultivating humility. Providing support for this, researchers at McGill University and the University of Quebec at Montreal (Lekes, Hope, Gouveia, Koestner, & Philippe, 2012) recently found that people engaged in written reflection exercises about their intrinsic values (as opposed to extrinsic values) prioritized intrinsic over extrinsic values and experienced greater well-being. Researchers have also demonstrated that people engaged in death reflections experienced greater feelings of gratitude compared to those that did not engage in such reflections (Frias, Watkins, Webber, & Froh, 2011). Although more empirical research is needed to determine the value of reflective practice in the development of humility, we believe that making time for reflection enables one to better understand strengths and weakness, one's interdependence with others, and the needs within the organization or opportunities within the organization for making a difference (transcendence). Exercises 3 and 4 provide interventions to lead you in reflection.

Exercise 3—Feedback Analysis

Feedback analysis was recommended by Peter Drucker, the famous management expert, to help people identify their strengths so that they may focus on strengths (rather than weaknesses) and experience excellence. Feedback analysis begins by writing down what you expect to happen and regularly reviewing the actual results to see if they match your original expectations. Then, use this information to help you determine areas of strength and weakness. Loosely based on this idea, we have developed the worksheet below to aid leaders in the process of discovering and sharing strengths and weaknesses. This exercise is extremely helpful in discovering strengths and weaknesses for the development of humility.

The Feedback Analysis Sheet

Describe the decision that was made: _____

Follow the completion of the exercise with a written reflection. While writing, think about the following questions:

- Based on the results of the decision and the feedback I received, what conclusions can I draw about my strengths and weaknesses?
- What are my next steps as a result of this feedback?
- How do I feel about the information I learned? Were there any surprises?
- Do I feel safe enough to move forward in this knowledge or prone to cover up my weaknesses? How can I move myself into a place where I feel safe to own or share my weaknesses?

TABLE 9.1 Feedback analysis

	Expected	Actual
Outcome of decision		
Completion date		
Self-assessment: What behaviors/behavioral tendencies will/did facilitate outcome attainment?		
Self-assessment: What behaviors/behavioral tendencies will/did inhibit outcome attainment?		
Other-assessment★: What behaviors/behavioral tendencies will/did facilitate outcome attainment?		
Other-assessment★: What behaviors/behavioral tendencies will/did inhibit outcome attainment?		

★ Others should include people who: 1) know you well enough to provide some assistance in thinking about your behavioral tendencies; 2) are involved in the decision and/or outcome who can observe what is actually going on; and 3) understand the purpose of the exercise is to help you identify your strengths and weaknesses (especially strengths) to aid in your personal and professional development.

Look carefully at the last bullet point on the sheet. What do we mean by safety? Because of the importance of safety to both exercising humility in general and specifically engaging in feedback analysis where weaknesses may be uncovered, we now define and discuss identity threat to explain the necessity of safety. Petriglieri (2011, p. 641) defines identity threat as "experiences appraised as indicating potential harm to the value, meanings, or enactment of an identity." So, imagine a time when you felt that just being you, acting as yourself was under attack. At that time, your identity was threatened. Admitting weakness, for many people, creates a situation where their identities feel threatened. However, as we have discussed in previous chapters, humility is not the same as feeling insignificant or ashamed of your weaknesses. It is extremely important that you hold on to that because when identities feel threatened, people tend to feel insignificant or worthless, and they often defend themselves (Peterson & Seligman, 2004), so instead of acting humbly, may behave arrogantly or ruthlessly. Therefore, in the written reflection, we specifically want you to think about the extent to which you feel safe or scared of the feedback you receive. If you feel scared, please counter these feelings with a reflection on your strengths. They may not be in the same arena in which you assessed feedback on your weaknesses, but you do have strengths. Think about where these strengths are manifest. A second table that we have developed can be used to aid your reflection and is provided below. The purpose of this table is to help you recalibrate and more deeply reflect on what might be a skill deficiency (a weakness that can be corrected through study, diligence, etc.) and a talent deficiency (an area of weakness that can be nominally corrected). We all have strengths and weaknesses. When we exercise humility, we correct the skill deficiencies and find ways to make up for talent deficiencies.

Exercise 4—Keep a Learning Diary

In Ignatian pedagogy, reflection is "a formative and a liberating process that forms the conscience of learners in such a manner that they are led to move beyond

TABLE 9.2 Skill deficiencies

Problem Area	What kind of deficiency is it?	How does it impede my performance?	What is your plan of action?
Have problems balancing a ledger	Skill deficiency	Not meeting job expectations	Take a course at the community college
Envisioning the future	Talent deficiency	Causing my team to get mired in the weeds rather than thinking big	Recruit people on the team who are conceptual thinkers

knowing to undertake action" (Korth, 2008, p. 282). When one thinks about reflection in this way, one is moved to journal. That is to create a time each day to write and thoughtfully consider experiences so that one can learn and move beyond knowing to action. Many people already keep journals for various purposes. We suggest you keep one specifically for the purposes of developing your capability to lead with humility. Based on what we've learned regarding reflection from the Jesuits, this journal should involve your reflections on your role as a leader and your interactions with followers. Consider the following questions for this journal:

- Who were the parties in the interaction?
- What was the substance of the interaction?
- What outcomes resulted or are expected to result from the interaction?
- What insight do you have about the interaction and about yourself in the interaction? Did you act with humility? How do you know?
- How did you look beyond your self-interests? That is, were you considering the interests of others? Were you focused on the transcendent vision?
- What should you work on to better demonstrate humility in future interactions?

Engaging in Behavioral Practices—Relational and Perspective Taking Leadership Activities

Behavioral practice simply means that you become engaged in actions that challenge you to act with humility. At this point, you have engaged in activities that put you in a relational mindset and you have reflected on your behavior and experiences. Now, we ask you to act with humility. This may feel exhilarating or a little uncomfortable at first. We want to encourage you. It *can* be exhilarating to take actions that cultivate your humility. However, if it feels challenging, keep doing the exercises below and like physical exercise, some of these will become easier with time.

Exercise 5—Practice Self-sacrifice

In Chapter 7, we introduced Bill Pollard of ServiceMaster. Although he was taking a senior executive job, he chose to act as a janitor and learn to clean carpets. In this exercise, you are going to do the same. The point of this exercise is to take the place of a subordinate, client, student (if you're a teacher), etc. It will be tempting to commit to one day or just a few hours of practicing self-sacrifice. We ask that you truly take on the role for a significant period of time. Don't show up and simply ask people what they do. Instead, put on your dungarees and get your hands dirty. Do their work or experience what they experience for a week or longer if you can. Your goal is to see and understand the experience of others by becoming the "other."

As you engage in the exercise, reflect (perhaps in writing) on the following:

- What am I asking people to do? What legitimate concerns and issues may be raised by the realization of the vision? How do I deal with these issues?
- Now that I am in the field, have I discovered that there are relevant points of view that I have failed to include in my thinking?
- What new information (if any) has this experience brought me about my strengths and weaknesses as a leader of my followers?
- How can I develop more meaningful relationships with my followers?

Exercise 6—Active Listening

Leaders who act with humility listen to others. They can then understand strengths and weaknesses, build stronger relationships with people, and ensure that the messages they send are properly understood. Active listening provides leaders the opportunity to truly hear feedback on their own strengths and weaknesses from others. Some of you may have experienced an active listening role play in a classroom. We think that is wonderful practice. Now we ask that you put this into action with the people with whom you work. David Kolb, Joyce Oslund, and Irwin Rubin (1995) provide excellent guidelines for active listening such as not judging, and reflecting back the actual content as well as the feelings and implications of content shared and, finally, inviting more communication. We provide some additional ways of thinking about these guidelines in the context of humble leadership.

- As a humble leader who is looking for feedback on strengths and weaknesses, you have to be sure that people feel you are an appreciative listener. Therefore, as people share their concerns, ideas, and thoughts about the vision (or about you), be sure to communicate that you are interested and open.
- Be sure to reflect content and implications of content. As you are engaging in visioning, someone may communicate their concerns about the vision or the difficulty of its implementation. At such a time, be sure to reflect that you heard both the concerns and the implications. For example, you might say something like, "So that may lead to a situation where people have to work extra hours for perhaps little tangible results?"
- Reflect the feelings behind the content—even if they reflect on your strengths and weaknesses as a leader. This guideline tries to surface some of the under-lying feeling that the speaker has not fully expressed. However, your role is not to tell people how they feel, but to try to understand how they feel. Continuing with our example above suppose the follower said, "Exactly, this plan could lead to lots of extra working hours for our group but not for any-one else. Senior Management always seems to dump on our group." You might respond, "If I were working extra hours but felt no one else was

sharing in the sacrifice, I'd feel frustrated." The natural tendency is to defend oneself by saying something like: "I'm not dumping on your group. Everyone is making sacrifices. In fact, just the other day . . . " Avoid this type of answer. Reflect the feelings—even if your identity feels a bit threatened.

If you feel that you haven't really understood or heard enough to reflect back feelings or implications, then you might simply say, "Tell me a bit more about that." This is a response we use often in our classrooms to understand and answer the questions that students ask. We also think this may be helpful if you feel just a bit overwhelmed or unsafe. Letting people talk more may uncover the root issues and give you a safer place from which to listen.

Think of a "listening posture" as part of your role. A relational orientation says that you judge yourself by the extent to which you fulfill your relationship roles. So, think of non-verbals that show that you are listening and interested as part of your relationship contract.

The great thing about developing active listening is that we can get plenty of practice, if we want. We are involved in interpersonal communications with our spouses, children, neighbors, and others constantly. So, the next time you're standing at the sink washing dishes and your significant other shares their day with you, listen actively. You may find it improves more than your work leadership skills.

Closing Thoughts

Cultivating humility in leadership involves preparing your heart, hands, and mind to become a different kind of leader, one who recognizes their strengths and weaknesses, has a vision larger than themselves, engages in self-sacrifice in such a way that followers see humility and are motivated to follow your leadership and similarly exhibit humility. While the six exercises in this chapter can be very helpful, we hope the real take-away from this chapter is that you can cultivate and develop your ability to exhibit humility. However, it requires intentionality, a relational identity orientation, reflection, and practice.

CASE STUDY: CAN HUMILITY REALLY BE DEVELOPED?

Can Organizations Encourage the Exercise of Humble Leadership?

In many ways, the question "can humility be developed" is essential to the study of leadership. William Byron of the Society of Jesus (2011) asked a similar question in a paper recently and invoked the term "humbition," which he defines as "an amalgam of humility and the magis (the Latin word Ignatius used to describe the extra effort, the greater reach expected of those who follow Christ)" (p. 3). We found this intriguing and sought to understand the origin of the term. Some seem to credit Jane Harper, a 30-year veteran of IBM, with coining the term. For example, William Taylor, of *Businessweek*, says Harper discusses humbition thusly:

> subtle blend of humility and ambition that drives the most successful leaders – an antidote to the know-it-all-hubris that affects so many business stars. "The more I know," she says sensibly, "the more I know there is to know."
>
> *(Taylor, 2008)*

Harper doesn't just talk about humbition, she integrated it into the socialization process of IBM. Specifically, Harper's role at IBM was to make it an organization that was attractive to young talent. However, in the early 1990s, IBM was considered an old, staid company—not a place for gifted young people. Harper made it her mission to change all of that by starting Extreme Blue, an internship program focused on luring stellar employees to IBM. Taylor and LaBarre (2006, p. 194) describe it as "MTV's Real World meets the Manhattan Project – groups of smart, young, ambitious people, living and working in close quarters, under intense pressure, focused on projects with huge potential." You would think that such a program would be extremely competitive with people trying to outperform one another. Our typical way of thinking about the development of young leaders is to throw them into tournament style, dog-eat-dog competitions and see who wins. In opposition to conventional wisdom, Harper strove for teamwork. According to Taylor:

> Harper and her colleagues have even produced a manual, called "Staying Extreme," that teaches young hotshots how (and how not) to get things done: "When you leave Extreme Blue and join another group at IBM (or any other company for that matter) . . . we will be watching. And if we find out that you are making the program look like

we are producing a bunch of arrogant wanna-be's, we will forget we ever knew you. Be ambitious. Be a leader. But do not belittle others in your pursuit of your ambitions."

(Taylor, 2008)

Moreover, Harper demonstrates humility when she talks about herself. When asked about great ideas in a 2000 interview, she stated that "great ideas come from great people" (Lanye, 2000) but went on to say that she isn't really a person who has great ideas; instead, her strength is her ability to identify great talent and help talented people bring their ideas to fruition. Has Harper been successful? The results speak for themselves. Extreme Blue attracts hundreds of sponsors and mentors each year. Eighty percent of the program's interns elect to work for IBM despite offers from companies like Google. More importantly, each summer more than 100 patent disclosures are filed by student interns. The company is attracting the best and the brightest, but not because they created a cut-throat internship program. It's because they attract people to the idea of ambitious humility—people working together to achieve important outcomes.

For your consideration, we offer the following questions:

- Is the Extreme Blue program able to help build "humbition"?
- What information influences your thinking on this question? What other information might be helpful?

10

PROGRESS NOT PERFECTION

The first responsibility of a leader is to define reality. The last is to say thank you. In between, the leader is a servant.

Max DePree, businessman and writer

We've discussed a number of leadership behaviors and provided compelling exemplars. As we near the end of this book, we'd like to dispel one final myth—leaders that display humility are perfect beings. In truth, any leader discussed in this book could be indicted tomorrow. You might find out that someone we've discussed was mean behind closed doors or has had an affair or ... well, the list could go on. So, let us just say it again, leaders who exercise humility are not perfect. We dispel this myth by considering two important ideas. First, character traits, like humility, appear in varying degrees. For example, Anil and Courtney are conscientious. However, Anil may be *more* conscientious than Courtney. Anil's conscientiousness does not diminish Courtney's conscientiousness. Similarly, some leaders are extremely humble while others are simply humble. So, if you're thinking, "I could never be Gandhi," we would simply reply that you don't have to be Gandhi to be humble. Second, we argue that leaders do not have to exhibit *every* virtue in order for them to be humble. For example, self-control is a character virtue as well as humility. Does the leader that acts with humility always exhibit self-control? Should we remove leaders from our book if we find an instance of the leader *not* exhibiting self-control? No, indeed, the inability to exhibit self-control may be one of the weaknesses to which the leader must admit.

The leaders we discuss in this book are exemplars because they are progressing toward humility. Like the asymptote, they are ever moving toward the straight line though they have not achieved perfection. They are *becoming* more humble leaders although they may fail or excel in exercising behaviors that signal humility at different times. So what about you? How can you progress toward humility? And, what will you do when, lo and behold, you discover your many imperfections in the exercise of humility? In this conclusion, we reinforce and extend three ideas found throughout this book.

Face Your Humanity

Throughout this book, we've reminded you that humble leaders acknowledge their strengths and weaknesses. Let us provide you with the first weakness to which you must admit: you are an imperfect human being. As a humble leader, you will do many things well and yet you will also stumble—perhaps badly at times. For example, you may be great at self-sacrifice but struggle notably at sharing weaknesses. You may be wonderful at transcendence but hate the idea of sacrificing your perks. Voltaire is quoted as saying "perfection is the enemy of the good." Please do not allow your humanity to get in the way of exercising humility—as you understand and can exercise it today. In the book, *Common Fire* (Daloz, Keen, Keen, & Parks, 1996), the authors interview a wide range of leaders who are committed to accomplishing good in the world. Yet, each of these leaders acknowledged motivations that others might consider suspect such as a desire for power, anger, or guilt. The authors found that the leaders discussed the necessity of inner conversations where one concedes and interrogates suspect motivations rather than shutting them out or pretending they do not exist. We go even further and say that accepting your humanity and confronting these motivations is the only way to prevent them from taking over because by acknowledging your humanity you can put these motivations in their proper place—the background.

Permit the Humanity of Others

When we talked with people about writing this book, we would mention the names of leaders that met our definition of humility such as Martin Luther King, Mother Teresa, and Jesus Christ—only to be told those people aren't *really* humble (yes, including Jesus). Obviously, we disagree with these critics and reiterate that perfection is not a requirement for humble leadership. Indeed, because there are no perfect human beings, we fear that this emphasis on perfection precludes anyone as a model from which we may learn. We encourage you to get over the idea that the people around you and even other leaders must be perfect. If you can't permit the humanity of others, you'll never be able to lead with humility. Leading with humility requires that you acknowledge your strengths and weaknesses and that you do the same for your followers. The authors of *Common Fire* state:

> Committed citizens seem to know that forgiveness and transformation are one and the same, and you can't be about the work of transforming society without a robust capacity to forgive—both yourself and others.
>
> *(Daloz et al., 1996, p. 192)*

Because leaders are those who are committed to bringing about change (within organizations or society), we encourage you to be prepared to allow for the humanity of others, to be prepared for their mistakes and lack of perfection just as you are prepared for your own.

Stay Focused on Relationships

Remember that leadership is a communal property. So, if you have lost the trust of your followers then you are no longer a leader. Stay focused on your relationships with them. Keep in mind that a relational identity orientation is evidenced when the self-definition is characterized by concern for the welfare of others and comparisons of actual performance to agreed upon role requirements (Brickson & Brewer, 2001). This means that when you possess a relational identity orientation, you will evaluate your performance in terms of your skill in performing interpersonal roles, focusing on cooperative interdependence and recognizing that your well-being is intricately linked to the well-being of your followers. Consequently, it is extremely important for you to ask followers for feedback and, at times, their forgiveness. Humility is demonstrated, in part, by keeping your eye on relationships.

Embrace Failure

We don't mean to suggest that you should fail willingly. We simply mean that a failure is as instructive as a success—perhaps more so. A. G. Lafley, former Proctor and Gamble CEO, says:

> My experience is that we learn much more from failure than we do success. Look at great politicians and successful sports teams. Their biggest lessons come from their toughest losses. The same is true for any kind of leader.
>
> *(Dillon, 2011, p. 86)*

In Chapter 9, we encouraged you to perform feedback analysis to help you cultivate humility in leadership. As we close the book, we highlight again that feedback analysis surfaces successes and failures for the purposes of better understanding strengths and weaknesses. But, Lafley goes on to say that it isn't enough to acknowledge failures: you have to learn from them. Similarly, we say humility is not evidenced by people who can simply perform feedback analysis, but by those who can learn from the strengths and weaknesses they discover. We think that an outgrowth of really learning from failure is the development of interdependence. What does this mean? Imagine you are a leader that fails in accomplishing a vision. Perhaps you want to get the people on your street to be more involved in keeping the streets clean and safe. You walk around to every door in the neighborhood and get people excited about the possibility of forming a network of homeowners committed to the health of the community. However, you find that fewer and fewer people attend each meeting because you get meeting notices out late or send the wrong dates or fail to follow up on issues mentioned in the meeting. Nothing is changing and people are discouraged. Was your failure in the vision? No, your failure was in the follow through because your weakness is in your attention to detail. Having had this experience, you may recognize the importance of bringing someone alongside you who can devote themselves to the details that make realizing the vision possible.

But, you say, I'm not really the leader. I'm just another person in the group, another team member. What can I do? Debra Meyerson, professor at Stanford's School of Education, researched a form of leadership called tempered radicalism. She says it is "more localized, more diffuse, more modest, and less visible than traditional forms— yet no less significant" (Meyerson, 2001, p. 93). Heifetz (1994) suggests that we think of leadership as an activity and anyone, at any level, can mobilize others to face pressing problems that need real solutions. We encourage you to engage in leadership by exercising humility. Be a tempered radical. For example, you know that norms within your team have been violated by just about everyone in the team. As a result, meetings rarely start on time, the tone is argumentative rather than constructive, and the team is in danger of not meeting the client or organizational objectives. You are not the team leader but you know that something has to change in order for the team to work together, to salvage relationships, and to meet objectives. Therefore, you might seize an opportunity to exercise leadership during an update meeting where it becomes clear that short-term objectives have not been met. First, you might admit that you've been part of the problem (came late to meetings, let a milestone slip, was defensive, etc.) and then reiterate the interdependence of group members. Next, you might suggest establishing and committing to norms. While you aren't the appointed team leader, such actions would demonstrate humble leadership.

Our Last Admonition: Learn, Struggle, and Grow

Simply, be encouraged that despite any failures, lows, and setbacks you may experience as you attempt to exercise humility in leadership, there is still great potential for you to exercise effective humble leadership. Engage in self-reflection often. Question yourself: Am I acknowledging my weaknesses *and* strengths? Am I demonstrating, voicing, and accepting my interdependence with others? Have I become passionate about a vision greater than myself? Don't be immobilized by fear of failure or even fear of not acting humbly. Commit today to leading with humility.

> Until one is committed, there is hesitancy, the chance to draw back— Concerning all acts of initiative (and creation), there is one elementary truth that ignorance of which kills countless ideas and splendid plans: that the moment one definitely commits oneself, then Providence moves too. All

sorts of things occur to help one that would never otherwise have occurred. A whole stream of events issues from the decision, raising in one's favor all manner of unforeseen incidents and meetings and material assistance, which no man could have dreamed would have come his way. Whatever you can do, or dream you can do, begin it. Boldness has genius, power, and magic in it. Begin it now.

Lee, n.d.

APPENDIX: DIAGNOSTIC SURVEY FOR HUMILITY

The inventory assessment items below were created by us and represent a subset of those we've used in our study of humility. We provide them to you in hopes that they may help you discover the extent to which you exhibit traits and/or behaviors associated with humility.

As you respond to each item, be honest with yourself. Although you may *intend* to exhibit a behavior or trait in the future, respond to the item based on who you are and how you behave *today*. Once you have completed the survey, use the scoring key provided to assess which dimensions of humility you are currently exhibiting.

Rating Scale

1   strongly disagree
2   disagree
3   slightly disagree
4   slightly agree
5   agree
6   strongly agree

TABLE A.1 Diagnostic survey for humility

Item	Rating					
1. I seek out the truth about myself, even if it highlights my weaknesses.	1	2	3	4	5	6
2. I identify the contributions and inherent worth of others around me.	1	2	3	4	5	6
3. I view myself as a good partner to those with which I interact (family members, co-workers, friends).	1	2	3	4	5	6
4. I am open to new information about myself.	1	2	3	4	5	6
5. I am aware that others have contributed to my accomplishments.	1	2	3	4	5	6
6. I view myself as a good member to a larger community (my local community, my workplace, groups to which I belong).	1	2	3	4	5	6
7. I do not react defensively towards criticism.	1	2	3	4	5	6
8. I appreciate the reality of being one person in a larger community.	.1	2	3	4	5	6
9. What is important to me is working to improve the welfare of the community(ies) I value and/or belong to (my local community, my workplace, groups to which I belong).	1	2	3	4	5	6
10. I actively seek out information about my strengths.	1	2	3	4	5	6
11. My accomplishments don't make me more valuable than others	.1	2	3	4	5	6
12. I feel my fate is intertwined with the fate of those around me.	1	2	3	4	5	6
13. I actively seek out information about my weaknesses.	1	2	3	4	5	6
14. I feel connected to a purpose greater than myself.	1	2	3	4	5	6
15. I feel good when I cooperate with others.	1	2	3	4	5	6

Scoring

Understanding yourself: #1, 4, 7, 10, 13
Relating to others: #3, 6, 9, 12, 15
Perspective: #2, 5, 8, 11, 14

Add together the numbers you choose for the "understanding yourself" items *only* (#1, 4, 7, 10, 13). Now, add together the numbers you chose for the "relating to others" items *only* (#3, 6, 9, 12, 15). Finally, add together numbers you chose for the "perspective" items *only* (#2, 5, 8, 11, 14). The interpretations of the scores are for each dimension of humility (understanding yourself, relating to others, perspective) rather than for humility as a whole. In this way, the measure gives you the opportunity to pinpoint where you wish to work to further develop your ability to exercise humility.

Interpretation

If you scored 0–10 on any dimension, you are *low* on this dimension. You'll want to go to Chapter 9 and think about the exercises that would be most helpful in cultivating that dimension of humility.

If you scored 11–20 on any dimension, you are *medium* on this dimension. For example, this means that you are sometimes exhibiting "understanding yourself" and sometimes you are not. To further develop your humility, you might try to understand the conditions that encourage you to exhibit the dimension and those that do not. First, go to Chapters 4, 5, and 6 for more information on each dimension. Then, go to Chapter 9 and see what exercises might be helpful in furthering your journey toward exercising humility.

If you scored 21–30 on any dimension, you are *high* on this dimension. For example, this means that you generally exercise "understanding yourself." To further develop your humility, you might try to understand how others perceive your leadership. Give this assessment to someone you trust to give you honest feedback and better understand if humility is being attributed to you (see Chapter 7 for more information on attributions of humility).

REFERENCES

Alcoholics Anonymous (1976). *Alcoholics Anonymous* (3rd ed.). New York, NY: Alcoholics Anonymous World Services.

Alcoholics Anonymous. (1980). *Dr. Bob and the good oldtimers: A biography, with recollections of early A.A. in the Midwest*. New York, NY: Alcoholics Anonymous World Services.

Alcoholics Anonymous (1981). *Twelve steps and twelve traditions*. New York, NY: Alcoholics Anonymous World Services.

Amason, A. (1996). Distinguishing effects of functional and dysfunctional conflict on strategic decision making: Resolving a paradox for top management teams. *Academy of Management Journal, 39*, 123–148. doi: 10.2307/256633

Ambition (n.d.). Merriam-Webster's online dictionary. Retrieved from http://www.merriam-webster.com/dictionary/ambition

American Psychiatric Association (1994). *Diagnostic and statistical manual of mental disorders* (4th ed.). Washington, DC: American Psychiatric Association.

"Are alpha males healthy?" (2011, September 13). *The Wall Street Journal*. Retrieved from http://online.wsj.com/article/SB10001424053111903532804576566553268698820.html

Ash, M. K. (1984). *Mary Kay on people management*. New York, NY: Warner Books.

Asplund, J., Lopez, S. J., Hodges, T., & Harter, J. (2009). The Clifton StrengthsFinder® 2.0 technical report: Development and validation. *Gallup Consulting*. Retrieved from http://strengths.gallup.com/private/Resources/CSFTechnicalReport031005.pdf

Atwater, L. E., & Yammarino, F. J. (1992). Does self-other agreement on leadership perceptions moderate the validity of leadership and performance predictions? *Personnel Psychology, 45*, 141–164. doi: 10.1111/j.1744-6570.1992.tb00848.x

Avolio, B. J., & Mhatre, K. H. (2012). Advances in theory and research on authentic leadership. In K. S. Cameron, & G. Spreitzer (Eds.), *The Oxford handbook of positive organizational scholarship* (pp. 773–783). Oxford: Oxford University Press.

Baker, A., & Stier, E. (2011, February 16). The woman at the head of Yemen's protest movement. *Time*. Retrieved from http://www.time.com/time/world/article/0,8599,2049476,00.html

Bandura, A. (1986). *Social foundations of thought and action: A social cognitive theory*. Englewood Cliffs, NJ: Prentice-Hall.

Bandura, A. (1997). *Self-efficacy: The exercise of control*. New York, NY: Freeman.

Bass, B. M., & Bass, R. (2008). *The Bass handbook of leadership: Theory, research, and managerial applications* (4th ed.). New York, NY: Free Press.

Bazerman, M. H., & Moore, D. A. (2008). *Judgment in managerial decision making* (7th ed.). Hoboken, NJ: John Wiley & Sons, Inc.

Bird, A. (2010). Leading through values: An interview with Paul Polmaan of Unilever. *Mckinsey Quarterly, 1*, 97–101.

Bond, M. H., Leung, K., & Wan, K. C. (1982). The social impact of self-effacing attributions: The Chinese case. *Journal of Social Psychology, 118*, 157–166. doi: 10.1080/00224545. 1982.9922794

Boundaoui, A. (2011, December 9). Tawakul Karman – Nobel Prize winner from Yemen. *The World*. Boston, MA: BBC. Retrieved from http://www.theworld.org/2011/12/tawakul-karman-nobel-prize-winner-from-yemen

Brickson, S., & Brewer, M. B. (2001). Identity orientation and intergroup relations in organizations. In M. A. Hogg, & D. J. Terry (Eds.), *Social identity processes in organizational contexts* (pp. 49–65). Philadelphia, PA: Psychology Press.

Buckingham, M., & Clifton, D. O. (2001). *Now, discover your strengths*. New York, NY: Free Press.

Byron, W. J. (2011). Humility, magis, and discernment: A Jesuit perspective on education for business leadership. *Journal of Jesuit Business Education, 2*(1), 9–20.

Capra, F., (Producer & Director) (1946). *It's a Wonderful Life* [Motion Picture]. USA. Liberty Films II. Retrieved from http://www.finestquotes.com/movie_quotes/movie/Its%20 a%20Wonderful%20Life/page/0.ht m#ixzz29TjFC8Bq

Choi, Y., & Mai-Dalton, R. R. (1998). On the leadership function of self-sacrifice. *Leadership Quarterly, 9*(4), 475. doi: 10.1016/S1048-9843(98)90012-1

Cialdini, R. B. & DeNicholas, M. E. (1989). Self-presentation by association. *Journal of Personality and Social Psychology, 57*, 626–632. doi: 10.1037/0022-3514.57.4.626

Clark, A. J. (2010). Empathy and sympathy: Therapeutic distinctions in counseling. *Journal of Mental Health Counseling, 32*, 95–101.

Collins, J. C. (2001). *Good to great: Why some companies make the leap—and others don't*. New York, NY: HarperBusiness.

Conger, J. A., & Kanungo, R. N. (1988). The empowerment process: Integrating theory and practice. *Academy of Management Journal, 13*, 471–482.

Dahlsgaard, K., Peterson, C., & Seligman, M. E. P. (2005). Shared virtue: The convergence of valued human strengths across culture and history. *Review of General Psychology, 9*, 203–213. doi: 10.1037/1089-2680.9.3.203

Daloz, L. A. P., Keen, C. H., Keen, J. P., & Parks, S. D. (1996). *Common fire: Leading lives of commitment in a complex world*. Boston, MA: Beacon Press.

Davidson, M. N. (2011). *The end of diversity as we know it*. San Francisco CA: Berrett-Koehler Publishers, Inc.

Davis, R., & Shrader, A. (2007). *Leading for growth: How Umpqua Bank got cool and created a culture of greatness*. San Francisco CA: Jossey-Bass.

Decety, J. & Moriguchi, Y. (2007). The empathic review brain and its dysfunction in psychiatric populations: Implications for intervention across different clinical conditions. *BioPsychoSocial Medicine, 1*(22), 1–21. doi: 10.1186/1751-0759-1-22

De Cremer, D., Van Dijke, M., Mayer, D. M., Schouten, B. C., & Bardes, M. (2009). When does self-sacrificial leadership motivate prosocial behavior? It depends on followers' prevention focus. *Journal of Applied Psychology, 94*(4), 887–899. doi: 10.1037/a0014782

DeDreu, C. K. W. (2006). When too little or too much hurts: Evidence for a curvilinear relationship between task conflict and innovation in teams. *Journal of Management, 32*, 83–107. doi: 10.1177/0149206305277795

Dillon, K. (2011). I think of my failures as a gift. *Harvard Business Review, 89*(4), 86–89.

Drucker, P. F. (2005). Managing oneself. *Harvard Business Review, 83*(1), 100–109.

Duval, S., & Wicklund, R. A. (1972). *A theory of objective self-awareness.* New York, NY: Academic Press.

Ely, R. J., Meyerson, D. E., & Davidson, M. N. (2006). Rethinking political correctness. *Harvard Business Review, 84*(9), 78–87.

Emavardhana, T., & Tori, C. D. (1997). Changes in self-concept, ego defense mechanisms, and religiosity following seven-day vipassana meditation retreats. *Journal for the Scientific Study of Religion, 36*, 194–206. doi: 10.2307/1387552

Exline, J. J., & Geyer, A. L. (2004). Perceptions of humility: A preliminary study. *Self and Identity, 3*, 95–104. doi: 10.1080/13576500342000077

Flynn, F. J. (2005). Identity orientations and forms of social exchange in organizations. *Academy of Management Review, 30*(4), 737–750. doi: 10.5465/AMR.2005.18378875

Frias, A., Watkins, P. C., Webber, A. C., & Froh, J. J. (2011). Death and gratitude: Death reflection enhances gratitude. *Journal of Positive Psychology, 6*(2), 154–162. doi:10.1080/17439760.2011.558848

Fry, L.W. (2003). Toward a theory of spiritual leadership. *Leadership Quarterly, 14*, 693–727. doi: 10.1016/j.leaqua.2003.09.001

Galinsky, A. D., Magee, J. C., Gruenfeld, D. H., Whitson, J. A., & Liljenquist, K. A. (2008) Power reduces the press of the situation: Implications for creativity, conformity, and dissonance. *Journal of Personality and Social Psychology, 95*, 1,450–1,466. doi: 10.1037/a0012633

Galinsky, A. D., Magee, J. C., Inesi, M. E., & Gruenfeld, D. H. (2006). Power and perspectives not taken. *Psychological Science, 17*(12), 1,068–1,074. doi 10.1111/j.1467-9280.2006.01824.x

Galinsky, A. D., Wang, C. S., & Ku, G. (2008). Perspective-takers behave more stereotypically. *Journal of Personality and Social Psychology, 95*, 404–419. doi: 10.1037/0022-3514.95.2.404

Garvin, D. A., & Roberto, M. A. (2001). What you don't know about making decisions. *Harvard Business Review, 79*(8), 108–119.

Gehlbach, H., Brinkworth, M. E., & Ming-Te, W. (2012). The social perspective taking process: What motivates individuals to take another's perspective? *Teachers College Record, 114*(1), 1–29.

George, W. (2003). *Authentic leadership: Rediscovering the secret to creating lasting value.* San Francisco, CA: Jossey-Bass.

George, W. (2007). *True north: Discover your authentic leadership.* San Francisco. CA: Jossey-Bass.

Gerdes, K. E., Segal, E. A., & Lietz, C. A. (2010). Conceptualising and measuring empathy. *British Journal of Social Work, 40*, 2,326–2,343. doi: 10.1093/bjsw/bcq048

Gesquiere, L. R., Learn, N. H., Simao, M. C. M., Onyango, P. O., Alberts, & Altman, J. (2011). Life at the top: Rank and stress in wild male baboons. *Science, 333*, 357–360. doi: 10.1126/science.1207120

Gibbons, F. X. (1990). Self-attention and behavior: A review and theoretical update.

Advances in Experimental Social Psychology, 23, 249–286. doi: 10.1016/S0065-2601(08) 60321-4

Gist, M. (1989). The influence of training method on self-efficacy and idea generation among managers. *Personnel Psychology, 42,* 787–805. doi: 10.1111/j.1744-6570.1989. tb00675.x

Gordon, M. (2009). *Roots of empathy: Changing the world child by child.* New York, NY: The Experiment, LLC.

Greenleaf, R. K. (1991). *The servant as leader.* Indianapolis, IN: The Robert K. Greenleaf Center. [Originally published in 1970, by Robert K. Greenleaf.]

Grenberg, J. (2005). *Kant and the ethics of humility: A story of dependence, corruption and virtue.* New York, NY: Cambridge University Press. doi: 0.1017/CBO9780511627859

Grint, K. (2005). Leadership Ltd: White elephant to wheelwright. *Ivey Business Journal, 69*(3), 1–4.

Guardian. (2003, March 19). George Bush's address on the start of war. Retrieved from http://www.guardian.co.uk/world/2003/mar/20/iraq.georgebush

Hannah, S. T., Avolio, B. J., & Walumbwa, F. (2010). The influence of authentic leadership on follower behaviors: A three-study investigation. Unpublished manuscript.

Hardin, G. (1968). The tragedy of the commons. *Science, 162,* 1,243–1,248. doi: 10.1126/science.162.3859.1243

Hareli, S., & Weiner, B. (2000). Accounts for success as determinants of perceived arrogance and modesty. *Motivation & Emotion, 24,* 215–236. doi: 10.1023/A:1005666212320

Haselton, M. G., Nettle, D., & Andrews, P. W. (2005). The evolution of cognitive bias. In D. M. Buss (Ed.), *Handbook of evolutionary psychology* (pp. 724–746). Hoboken, NJ: Wiley.

Heifetz, R. A. (1994). *Leadership without easy answers.* Cambridge, MA: Belknap Press.

Heifetz, R. A., & Linsky, M. (2002). *Leadership on the line: Staying alive through the dangers of leading.* Boston, MA: Harvard Business School Press.

Hesselbein, F. (2011). *My life in leadership: The journey and lessons learned along the way.* San Francisco, CA: Jossey-Bass.

House, R. J., & Howell, J. M. (1992). Personality and charismatic leadership. *Leadership Quarterly, 3,* 81–108. doi: 10.1016/1048-9843(92)90028-E

Howard, A., & Wellins, R. S. (1994). High-involvement leadership: Changing roles for changing times. *Leadership Research Institute, Developmental Dimensions International.*

Hsieh, T. (2010). *Delivering happiness.* New York, NY: Business Plus.

Jehn, K. (1997). A qualitative analysis of conflict types and dimensions in organizational groups. *Administrative Science Quarterly, 42,* 530–557. doi: 10.2307/2393737

Jensen, S. M., & Luthans, F. (2006). Entrepreneurs as authentic leaders: Impact on employees' attitudes. *Leadership & Organization Development Journal, 27,* 646–666. doi: 10.1108/01437730610709273

Johnson, R. E., Silverman, S. B., Shyamsunder, A., Swee, H., Rodopman, O., Cho, E., & Bauer, J. (2010). Acting superior but actually inferior?: Correlates and consequences of workplace arrogance. *Human Performance, 23*(5), 403–427. doi: 10.1080/08959285. 2010.515279

Jones, E. E. & Wortman, C. (1973). *Ingratiation: An attributional approach.* Morristown, NJ: General Learning Press.

Judge, T. A., & Bono, J. E. (2000). Five-factor model of personality and transformational leadership. *Journal of Applied Psychology, 85,* 751–765. doi: 10.1037/0021-9010.85.5.751

Judge, T. A., Bono, J. E., Ilies, R., & Gerhardt, M. W. (2002). Personality and leadership:

A qualitative and quantitative review. *Journal of Applied Psychology*, 87, 765–780. doi: 10.1037/0021-9010.87.4.765

Kahneman, D., & Tversky, A. (1973). On the psychology of prediction. *Psychological Review*, 80, 237–251. doi: 10.1037/h0034747

King, Jr., M. L. K., & Carson, C. (Ed.). (2007). *The papers of Martin Luther King, Jr. Volume VI: Advocate of the social gospel: September 1948–March, 1963*. Berkeley, CA: University of California Press.

Kirkman, B. L., & Rosen, B. (1999). Beyond self-management: The antecedents and consequences of team empowerment. *Academy of Management Journal*, 42: 58–74. doi: 10.2307/256874

Kirkpatrick, S. A. (2009). Lead through vision and values. In E. A. Locke (Ed.), *Handbook of principles of organizational behavior: Indispensable knowledge for evidence based management* (pp. 367–388). Chichester: John Wiley & Sons.

Kolb, D. A., Osland, J. S., & Rubin, I. M. (1995). *Organizational behavior: An experiential approach* (6th ed.). Englewood Cliffs, NJ: Prentice Hall.

Korth, S. J. (2008). Precis of Ignatian pedagogy: A practical approach. In G. W. Traub (Ed.), *A Jesuit education reader* (pp. 280–284). Chicago, IL: Loyola Press.

Krishnamurthi, J. (2009, December 17). Only when one is as nothing. *J. Krishnaurthi online: The official repository of the authentic teaching of J. Krishnamurthi*. Retrieved from http://www.jkrishnamurti.org/krishnamurti-teachings/view-daily- quote/20091217.php?t=God

Lanye, A. (2000, April 30). Jane Harper. *Fast Company*. Retrieved from http://www.fastcompany.com/62712/jane-harper

Lawrence, P. (2008). Neohumility/humility and business leadership: Do they belong together? *Journal of Business and Leadership*, 2, 116–126.

Lee (n.d.). Until one is committed. In *Popular Quotes: Commitment*. Retrieved from http://www.goethesociety.org/pages/quotescom.html

Lekes, N., Hope, N. H., Gouveia, L., Koestner, R., & Philippe, F. L. (2012). Influencing value priorities and increasing well-being: The effects of reflecting on intrinsic values. *Journal of Positive Psychology*, 7(3), 249–261. doi: 10.1080/17439760.2012.677468

Leslie, S. G., & Aaker, J. (2010). Zappos: Happiness in a box. *Stanford GSB No. M-333*. Stanford, CA: Leland Stanford Junior University.

Maharaj, M., & Kathrada, A. M. (2006). *Mandela: The authorized portrait*. Kansas City, MO: Andrews McMeel Pub.

Maney, K. (2003, March 21). Tiny tech company awes viewers. *USA Today*. Retrieved from http://usatoday30.usatoday.com/tech/news/techinnovations/2003-03-20-earthviewer_x.htm

Martin, J. (2006). Reinterpreting internalization and agency through G. H. Mead's perspectival realism. *Human Development*, 49, 65–86. doi: 10.1159/000091333

Martin, J., Sokol, B. W., Elfers, T. (2008). Taking and coordinating perspectives: From prereflective interactivity, through reflective intersubjectivity, to metareflective sociality. *Human Development*, 51, 294–317. doi: 10.1159/000170892

McClelland, D. C., & Burnham, D. H. (1976). Power is the great motivator. *Harvard Business Review*, 54(2), 100–110.

McCullough, M. E., & Snyder, C. R. (2000). Classical sources of human strength: Revisiting an old home and building a new one. *Journal of Social and Clinical Psychology*, 19, 1–10. doi: 10.1521/jscp.2000.19.1.1

McGregor, J. (2011). The Costco king checks out. *Washington Post*. Retrieved from http://

www.washingtonpost.com/blogs/post-leadership/post/costco-ceo-jim-sinegal-checks-out/2011/04/01/gIQAh7CqwJ_blog.html

McRae, P. R., & Costa, Jr., P. T. (1991). Adding Liebe und Arbeit: The full five-factor model and well-being. *Personality & Social Psychology Bulletin, 17,* 227–232.

Meer, F. (1988). *Higher than hope: The authorized biography of Nelson Mandela.* New York, NY: Harper & Row Publishers.

Meyerson, D. E. (2001). Radical change, the quiet way. *Harvard Business Review, 79*(9), 92–100.

Milliman, J. F. & Neck, C. P. (1994). Thought leadership: Finding spiritual fulfillment in organizational life. *Journal of Managerial Psychology, 9*(6), 9–16. doi: 10.1108/02683949410070151

Morris, J. A., Brotheridge, C. M., & Urbanski, J. C. (2005). Bringing humility into leadership: Antecedents and consequences of leader humility. *Human Relations, 58,* 1,323–1,350. doi: 10.1177/0018726705059929

NCAA. (2012). Probability of competing in athletics beyond high school. National Collegiate Athletic Association. Retrieved from: http://www.ncaa.org/wps/wcm/connect/public/Test/Issues/Recruiting/Probability+of+Going+Pro

Nielsen, R., Marrone, J. A., & Slay, H. S. (2010). A new look at humility: Exploring the humility concept and its role in socialized charismatic leadership. *Journal of Leadership & Organizational Studies, 17,* 33–43. doi: 10.1177/1548051809350892

Owens, B. P., & Hekman, D. R. (2012). Modeling how to grow: An inductive examination of humble leader behaviors, contingencies, and outcomes. *Academy of Management Journal, 55,* 787–818. doi: 10.5465/amj.2010.0441

Pandya, M., & Shell, R. (2005). *Nightly business report presents lasting leadership: What you can learn from the top 25 business people of our times.* Upper Saddle River, NJ: Wharton School Pub.

Pearce, C. L., & Conger, J. A., (2003). *Shared leadership: Reframing the hows and whys of leadership.* Thousand Oaks, CA: Sage Publications.

Peterson, C., & Seligman, M. E. P. (Eds.) (2004). *Character strengths and virtues: A handbook and classification.* Oxford: Oxford University Press.

Petriglieri, J. L. (2011). Under threat: Responses to and the consequences of threats to individuals' identities. *Academy of Management Review, 36*(4), 641–662. doi: 10.5465/amr.2009.0087

Pickett, J. P. (Ed.). (2001). *The American heritage dictionary* (4th ed.). New York, NY: Dell.

Pink, D. H. (2011). *Drive: The surprising truth about what motivates us.* New York, NY: Riverhead Books.

Pollard, C. W. (1996). *The soul of the firm.* New York, NY: HarperBusiness.

Ratliff, E. (2007, June 26). Google maps is changing the way we see the world. *Wired.* Retrieved from http://www.wired.com/techbiz/it/magazine/15-07/ff_maps?currentPage=all

Reiss, S., & Wiltz, J. (2001, September 1). Why America loves reality TV. *Psychology Today.* Retrieved from http://www.psychologytoday.com/articles/200109/why-america-loves-reality-tv

Ridge, M. (2000). Modesty as a virtue. *American Philosophical Quarterly, 37,* 269–283.

Ryan, D. S. (1983). Self-esteem: An operational definition and ethical analysis. *Journal of Psychology and Theology, 11,* 295–302.

Sauer, S. J. (2011). Taking the reins: The effects of new leader status and leadership style on team performance. *Journal of Applied Psychology*, 96, 574–587. doi: 10.1037/a0022741

Sauer, S. J. (2012). Why bossy is better for rookie managers. *Harvard Business Review*, **90**(5), 30.

Saulsman, L. M., & Page, A. C. (2004). The five-factor model and personality disorder empirical literature: A meta-analytic review. *Clinical Psychology Review, 23*, 1,055–1,085. doi: 10.1016/j.cpr.2002.09.001

Seattle University. (n.d.). Mission, vision, & values. Retrieved from http://www.seattleu.edu/about/mission

Selman, R. L. (1980). *The growth of interpersonal understanding: Developmental and clinical analyses.* New York, NY: Academic Press.

Shedler, J., & Manis, M. (1986). Can the availability heuristic explain vividness effects? *Journal of Personality & Social Psychology, 51*, 26–36. doi: 10.1037/0022-3514.51.1.26

Silverman, S. B., Johnson, R. E., McConnell, N., & Carr, A. (2012). Arrogance: A formula for leadership failure. *The Industrial-Organizational Psychologist, 50*(1), 21–28.

Spears, L. (1996). Reflections on Robert K. Greenleaf and servant-leadership. *Leadership & Organization Development Journal, 17*(7), 33–35. doi: 10.1108/01437739610148367

Stogdill, R. M. (1948). Personal factors associated with leadership: A survey of the literature. *Journal of Psychology, 25*, 35–71. doi: 10.1080/00223980.1948.9917362

Swann Jr., W. B., Stein-Seroussi, A., & Giesler, R. (1992). Why people self-verify. *Journal of Personality & Social Psychology, 62*(3), 392–401. doi: 10.1037/0022-3514.62.3.392

Tangney, J. P. (2000). Humility: Theoretical perspectives, empirical findings and directions for future research. *Journal of Social and Clinical Psychology, 19,* 70–82. doi: 10.1521/jscp.2000.19.1.70

Tangney, J. P. (2002). Humility. In C. R. Snyder, & S. J. Lopez (Eds.), *Handbook of positive organizational psychology* (pp. 411–419). New York, NY: Oxford University Press.

Tawakkol Karman – Biographical (n.d.). Nobelprize.org. Retrieved from http://www.nobelprize.org/nobel_prizes/peace/laureates/2011/karman.html

Taylor, W. C. (2008, March 6). Talent and "humbition". *Bloomberg Businessweek*. Retrieved from http://www.businessweek.com/stories/2008-03-06/william-c-dot-taylor-talent-and-humbition-businessweek-business-news-stock-market-and-financial-advice

Taylor, W. C., & LaBarre, P. G. (2006). *Mavericks at work: Why the most original minds in business win.* New York, NY: William Morrow.

Trump, D. J., & Schwartz, T. (1987). *Trump: The art of the deal.* New York, NY: Random House, Inc.

Tutu, D. (2007). *Believe: The words and inspiration of Desmond Tutu.* Boulder, CO: Blue Mountain Press.

Tversky, A., & Kahneman, D. (1973). Availability: A heuristic for judging frequency and probability. *Cognitive Psychology, 4*, 207–232. doi: 10.1016/0010-0285(73)90033-9

Unilever. (n.d.). Unilever sustainable living plan. Rotterdam, Netherlands. Retrieved from http://www.unilever.com/images/UnileverSustainableLivingPlan_tcm13-284876.pdf

University of Pennsylvania (n.d.). Positive psychology executive summary. Retrieved from http://www.positivepsychology.org/executivesummary.htm

Uzoma, K. (2011, May 31). How much TV does the average child watch each day? Livestrong.com. Retrieved from http://www.livestrong.com/article/222032-how-much-tv-does-the-average-child-watch-each-day

van de Ven, A. H. (2001). Medtronic's chairman William George on how mission-driven companies create long-term shareholder value. *Academy of Management Executive, 15*(4), 39–47. doi:10.5465/AME.2001.5897653 van Dierendonck, D. (2011). Servant leadership: A review and synthesis. *Journal of Management, 37*, 1,228–1,261.

van Knippenberg, D., van Knippenberg, B., De Cremer, D., & Hogg, M. A. (2004). Leadership, self, and identity: A review and research agenda. *Leadership Quarterly, 15,* 825–856. doi: 10.1016/j.leaqua.2004.09.002

Vipassana meditation (n.d). The technique. Retrieved from http://www.dhamma.org/en/vipassana.shtml

Vipassana meditation course for business executives (n.d.). Retrieved from http://www.executive.dhamma.org/en

Wallis, C. (2005, January 17). The new science of happiness. *Time*, A3–A9.

Walumbwa, F. O., Avolio, B. J., Gardner, W. L., Wernsing, T. S., & Peterson, S. J. (2008). Authentic leadership: Development and validation of a theory-based measure. *Journal of Management, 34*, 89–126. doi: 10.1177/0149206307308913

Wilson, B. (1983). *A. A. Tradition: How it developed.* [Brochure.] New York, NY: A. A. World Services, Inc.

Woodcock, S. (2008). The social dimensions of modesty. *Canadian Journal of Philosophy, 38*(1), 1–30. doi: 10.1353/cjp.0.0009

Woodward, K. L., & Miller, S. (1994). What is virtue? *Newsweek, 123*(24), 38–39.

Wosinka, W., Dabul, A. J., Whetstone-Dion, R., & Cialdini, R. B. (1996). Self-presentational responses to success in organization: The costs and benefits of modesty. *Basic and Applied Psychology, 18*, 229–242. doi: 10.1207/s15324834basp1802_8

Yukl, G. (2006). *Leadership in Organizations* (6th ed.). Englewood Cliffs, NJ: Prentice Hall.

Yukl, G. (2013). *Leadership in Organizations* (8th ed.). Upper River Saddle, NJ: Pearson.

Yukl, G., Seifert, C. F., & Chavez, C. (2008). Validation of the extended influence behavior questionnaire. *Leadership Quarterly, 19*, 609–621. doi: 10.1016/j.leaqua.2008.07.006

INDEX